BEER
Tasting
NOTES

this notebook belongs to

_____

_____

_____

BEER
Tasting
NOTES

CICO BOOKS
LONDON NEW YORK

Published in 2013 by CICO Books
An imprint of Ryland Peters & Small Ltd

20–21 Jockey's Fields   519 Broadway, 5th Floor
London WC1R 4BW   New York, NY 10012

www.cicobooks.com

10 9 8 7 6 5 4 3 2 1

A CIP catalog record for this book is available from
the Library of Congress and the British Library.

ISBN: 978 1 908862 92 1

Design concept: Wide Open Studios
Designer: Jerry Goldie
Style photography: Gavin Kingcome
Motif illustration: Stephen Dew
Cover illustration: Wide Open Studios

For digital editions, visit
www.cicobooks.com/apps.php

Printed in China

Contents

PART ONE

Understanding
Beer

Beer Styles

Beer—one of history's finest inventions, one of life's greatest pleasures. Whoever worked out that mixing water, grain, and hops could produce something so magnificent really deserves a pat on the back.

Today, beer is in better shape than it has ever been with new breweries opening every week, headed by individuals driven by a passion for making outstanding beer rather than the desire to earn a quick buck. As of June 2012, in the US alone there are well over 2,000 breweries in business, the most since 1887. This means if every day you drank a beer made by a different brewery, it would take you over five years to get through them all. The story in the UK is similar, with the Campaign for Real Ale (Camra) stating that there are now 1,000 breweries in operation. More than there have been for 70 years. And the growth is not limited to these countries with a rich history of enjoying beer. Forward-thinking brewers are creating exciting beers in Brazil, Japan, Italy, Australia, Denmark, and New Zealand to name just a few.

With all these new beers coming to local bars and pubs, it means there is a lot of drinking to be done. And with so much choice, you need somewhere to keep a record of the good ones. That's where this journal comes in. Over the following pages you will find space you record your thoughts on well over 100 beers. With space to note the key characteristics—style, who brewed it, where it was from, the variety of hops used, etc—plus handy boxes to tick off the flavors you get from the beer, each page has been designed to offer the quickest and easiest way to make tasting notes, so as not to interupt you from enjoying your beer.

Here's a quick descriptions of some of the most popular styles and what to expect from them:

American IPAs

A direct descendent of the original Indian Pale Ale, this American version is the beer that really kickstarted the craft beer movement and helped seal the reputation of the US as a leader in contemporary brewing. What makes an American IPA instantly recognizable is the hit of the C-hops, such as Citra and Cascade, that give the beer its distinctive citrusy aroma. These beers are highly hopped, resulting in a very bitter finish, and brewers continue push up the level of hops to produce Double IPAs and Imperial IPAs that are testing the limits of even the most committed hop head.

Trappist and Abbey Beers

Not so much a beer style but more of a collective term to group several Belgian beer styles: Dubbel, Tripel, and Quadrupel. These names refer to the original gravity of the beer and its strength, with Dubbel being the weakest at around 7% ABV on average and Quadrupel the strongest at 10% or higher, sometimes even hitting the 14% mark. There is also a light Singel style but the monks tend to keep that one for themselves. To be a true Trappist beer, it must be brewed within the walls of a Trappist monastery, either by the monks themselves or by a brewer under their supervision. Any brewery that makes the same styles of beer as the monks but not in a monastery is said to produce Abbey beers.

Blonde and Golden Ales

Blonde ales are traditionally brewed at around 4.5–6% ABV and are low in bitterness, usually sticking to European hop varieties. A good Blonde will make for excellent summer drinking with a golden color, good amount of effervescence, and smooth, crisp finish.

Fruit Beers

Fruit beers originated in Belgium but have been truly embraced by the international craft beer community, who thrive on the challenge of experimenting with new ingredients. The classic ingredient is cherry, added to sour Lambic beers to produce Kriek, but modern breweries are throwing in whatever they can get their hands on in the forms of fruit juices and purées. Peach, raspberry, and strawberry are all popular additions, but look out for more unusual versions with blueberries, apricots, guava, pomegranate, and blackberries.

Bitters

Walk into any decent pub in the UK and you should be able to order a well-hopped, cask-conditioned beer between 3.5% and 5% ABV, served by the pint on draught. This is your classic bitter and is what UK pubs are famous for. The weaker versions tend to be classified as Bitters and the stronger examples are called Best Bitters, but both contain British hop varieties such as Fuggles and Goldings that give a moderate bitterness and dry finish.

Stouts and Porters

Porters and Stouts are easily identified by their dark coloring and burnt flavor thanks to the use of pale and black malts. Porters have evolved since their inception in 18th-century London and the modern version will have hints of coffee and chocolate, as well as dark fruits and a nuttiness that makes them suited to autumn and winter drinking. They are traditionally lighter, less full-bodied, and sweeter in flavor than Stouts, which have more pronounced dark chocolate and coffee characteristics thanks to the use of roasted malts. However, the differences  between the two styles are becoming increasingly blurred as brewers experiment with different combinations of hops and malts.

Pilsners

Though often poorly imitated—particularly by unscrupulous multinational breweries determined to remove any flavor from the beer—a good Pilsner is a drink to savor. Pale gold, bitter, and topped with a thick pillow of foam, it is a truly classic beer. The traditional Czech versions are golden, slightly sweet, and packed with floral aromas from the Saaz hops. The German ones tend to be lighter in color and have a more bitter finish.

Helles

This is a real Bavarian classic, found throughout the beer halls of Munich. It's a light, refreshing beer that's ideal for a summer drinking session. It is similar in color to its cousin, Pilsner, but packs less of a punch with lower bitterness, plus malt flavors and gentle floral aroma.

PART TWO

Tasting
Notes

**** 🍷 ****

TASTING NOTES

Name:

Brewery:

Country of origin:

Style:

Where sampled:

Hops:

ABV:

IBU/bitterness:

SRM/color:

Notes

Flavor profile:

- ☐ Sweet
- ☐ Sour
- ☐ Acidic
- ☐ Cask
- ☐ Keg
- ☐ Bottle

- ☐ Hoppy
- ☐ Bitter
- ☐ Yeasty
- ☐ Malty
- ☐ Wheat
- ☐ Spicy

- ☐ Weak
- ☐ Strong
- ☐ Full-bodied
- ☐ Watery
- ☐ Clean
- ☐ Balanced

- ☐ Clear
- ☐ Cloudy
- ☐ Light
- ☐ Dark
- ☐ Flat
- ☐ Fizzy

- ☐ Fruity
- ☐ Citrus
- ☐ Floral
- ☐ Chocolate
- ☐ Toffee
- ☐ Coffee

TASTING NOTES

Name:

Brewery:

Country of origin:

Style:

Where sampled:

Hops:

ABV:

IBU/bitterness:

SRM/color:

Notes

Flavor profile:

☐ Sweet	☐ Hoppy	☐ Weak	☐ Clear	☐ Fruity
☐ Sour	☐ Bitter	☐ Strong	☐ Cloudy	☐ Citrus
☐ Acidic	☐ Yeasty	☐ Full-bodied	☐ Light	☐ Floral
☐ Cask	☐ Malty	☐ Watery	☐ Dark	☐ Chocolate
☐ Keg	☐ Wheat	☐ Clean	☐ Flat	☐ Toffee
☐ Bottle	☐ Spicy	☐ Balanced	☐ Fizzy	☐ Coffee

TASTING NOTES

Name:

Brewery:

Country of origin:

Style:

Where sampled:

Hops:

ABV:

IBU/bitterness:

SRM/color:

Notes

Flavor profile:

- ☐ Sweet
- ☐ Sour
- ☐ Acidic
- ☐ Cask
- ☐ Keg
- ☐ Bottle

- ☐ Hoppy
- ☐ Bitter
- ☐ Yeasty
- ☐ Malty
- ☐ Wheat
- ☐ Spicy

- ☐ Weak
- ☐ Strong
- ☐ Full-bodied
- ☐ Watery
- ☐ Clean
- ☐ Balanced

- ☐ Clear
- ☐ Cloudy
- ☐ Light
- ☐ Dark
- ☐ Flat
- ☐ Fizzy

- ☐ Fruity
- ☐ Citrus
- ☐ Floral
- ☐ Chocolate
- ☐ Toffee
- ☐ Coffee

TASTING NOTES

Name:

Brewery:

Country of origin:

Style:

Where sampled:

Hops:

ABV:

IBU/bitterness:

SRM/color:

Notes

Flavor profile:

- ☐ Sweet
- ☐ Sour
- ☐ Acidic
- ☐ Cask
- ☐ Keg
- ☐ Bottle

- ☐ Hoppy
- ☐ Bitter
- ☐ Yeasty
- ☐ Malty
- ☐ Wheat
- ☐ Spicy

- ☐ Weak
- ☐ Strong
- ☐ Full-bodied
- ☐ Watery
- ☐ Clean
- ☐ Balanced

- ☐ Clear
- ☐ Cloudy
- ☐ Light
- ☐ Dark
- ☐ Flat
- ☐ Fizzy

- ☐ Fruity
- ☐ Citrus
- ☐ Floral
- ☐ Chocolate
- ☐ Toffee
- ☐ Coffee

TASTING NOTES

Name:

Brewery:

Country of origin:

Style:

Where sampled:

Hops:

ABV:

IBU/bitterness:

SRM/color:

Notes

Flavor profile:

- ☐ Sweet
- ☐ Sour
- ☐ Acidic
- ☐ Cask
- ☐ Keg
- ☐ Bottle

- ☐ Hoppy
- ☐ Bitter
- ☐ Yeasty
- ☐ Malty
- ☐ Wheat
- ☐ Spicy

- ☐ Weak
- ☐ Strong
- ☐ Full-bodied
- ☐ Watery
- ☐ Clean
- ☐ Balanced

- ☐ Clear
- ☐ Cloudy
- ☐ Light
- ☐ Dark
- ☐ Flat
- ☐ Fizzy

- ☐ Fruity
- ☐ Citrus
- ☐ Floral
- ☐ Chocolate
- ☐ Toffee
- ☐ Coffee

TASTING NOTES

Name:

Brewery:

Country of origin:

Style:

Where sampled:

Hops:

ABV:

IBU/bitterness:

SRM/color:

Notes

Flavor profile:

☐ Sweet	☐ Hoppy	☐ Weak	☐ Clear	☐ Fruity
☐ Sour	☐ Bitter	☐ Strong	☐ Cloudy	☐ Citrus
☐ Acidic	☐ Yeasty	☐ Full-bodied	☐ Light	☐ Floral
☐ Cask	☐ Malty	☐ Watery	☐ Dark	☐ Chocolate
☐ Keg	☐ Wheat	☐ Clean	☐ Flat	☐ Toffee
☐ Bottle	☐ Spicy	☐ Balanced	☐ Fizzy	☐ Coffee

TASTING NOTES

Name:

Brewery:

Country of origin:

Style:

Where sampled:

Hops:

ABV:

IBU/bitterness:

SRM/color:

Notes

Flavor profile:

☐ Sweet	☐ Hoppy	☐ Weak	☐ Clear	☐ Fruity
☐ Sour	☐ Bitter	☐ Strong	☐ Cloudy	☐ Citrus
☐ Acidic	☐ Yeasty	☐ Full-bodied	☐ Light	☐ Floral
☐ Cask	☐ Malty	☐ Watery	☐ Dark	☐ Chocolate
☐ Keg	☐ Wheat	☐ Clean	☐ Flat	☐ Toffee
☐ Bottle	☐ Spicy	☐ Balanced	☐ Fizzy	☐ Coffee

TASTING NOTES

Name:

Brewery:

Country of origin:

Style:

Where sampled:

Hops:

ABV:

IBU/bitterness:

SRM/color:

Notes

Flavor profile:

- ☐ Sweet
- ☐ Sour
- ☐ Acidic
- ☐ Cask
- ☐ Keg
- ☐ Bottle

- ☐ Hoppy
- ☐ Bitter
- ☐ Yeasty
- ☐ Malty
- ☐ Wheat
- ☐ Spicy

- ☐ Weak
- ☐ Strong
- ☐ Full-bodied
- ☐ Watery
- ☐ Clean
- ☐ Balanced

- ☐ Clear
- ☐ Cloudy
- ☐ Light
- ☐ Dark
- ☐ Flat
- ☐ Fizzy

- ☐ Fruity
- ☐ Citrus
- ☐ Floral
- ☐ Chocolate
- ☐ Toffee
- ☐ Coffee

TASTING NOTES

Name:

Brewery:

Country of origin:

Style:

Where sampled:

Hops:

ABV:

IBU/bitterness:

SRM/color:

Notes

Flavor profile:

☐ Sweet	☐ Hoppy	☐ Weak	☐ Clear	☐ Fruity
☐ Sour	☐ Bitter	☐ Strong	☐ Cloudy	☐ Citrus
☐ Acidic	☐ Yeasty	☐ Full-bodied	☐ Light	☐ Floral
☐ Cask	☐ Malty	☐ Watery	☐ Dark	☐ Chocolate
☐ Keg	☐ Wheat	☐ Clean	☐ Flat	☐ Toffee
☐ Bottle	☐ Spicy	☐ Balanced	☐ Fizzy	☐ Coffee

TASTING NOTES

Name:

Brewery:

Country of origin:

Style:

Where sampled:

Hops:

ABV:

IBU/bitterness:

SRM/color:

Notes

Flavor profile:

☐ Sweet	☐ Hoppy	☐ Weak	☐ Clear	☐ Fruity
☐ Sour	☐ Bitter	☐ Strong	☐ Cloudy	☐ Citrus
☐ Acidic	☐ Yeasty	☐ Full-bodied	☐ Light	☐ Floral
☐ Cask	☐ Malty	☐ Watery	☐ Dark	☐ Chocolate
☐ Keg	☐ Wheat	☐ Clean	☐ Flat	☐ Toffee
☐ Bottle	☐ Spicy	☐ Balanced	☐ Fizzy	☐ Coffee

TASTING NOTES

Name:

Brewery:

Country of origin:

Style:

Where sampled:

Hops:

ABV:

IBU/bitterness:

SRM/color:

Notes

Flavor profile:

▢ Sweet	▢ Hoppy	▢ Weak	▢ Clear	▢ Fruity
▢ Sour	▢ Bitter	▢ Strong	▢ Cloudy	▢ Citrus
▢ Acidic	▢ Yeasty	▢ Full-bodied	▢ Light	▢ Floral
▢ Cask	▢ Malty	▢ Watery	▢ Dark	▢ Chocolate
▢ Keg	▢ Wheat	▢ Clean	▢ Flat	▢ Toffee
▢ Bottle	▢ Spicy	▢ Balanced	▢ Fizzy	▢ Coffee

TASTING NOTES

Name:

Brewery:

Country of origin:

Style:

Where sampled:

Hops:

ABV:

IBU/bitterness:

SRM/color:

Notes

Flavor profile:

☐ Sweet	☐ Hoppy	☐ Weak	☐ Clear	☐ Fruity
☐ Sour	☐ Bitter	☐ Strong	☐ Cloudy	☐ Citrus
☐ Acidic	☐ Yeasty	☐ Full-bodied	☐ Light	☐ Floral
☐ Cask	☐ Malty	☐ Watery	☐ Dark	☐ Chocolate
☐ Keg	☐ Wheat	☐ Clean	☐ Flat	☐ Toffee
☐ Bottle	☐ Spicy	☐ Balanced	☐ Fizzy	☐ Coffee

TASTING NOTES

Name:

Brewery:

Country of origin:

Style:

Where sampled:

Hops:

ABV:

IBU/bitterness:

SRM/color:

Notes

Flavor profile:

- ☐ Sweet
- ☐ Sour
- ☐ Acidic
- ☐ Cask
- ☐ Keg
- ☐ Bottle

- ☐ Hoppy
- ☐ Bitter
- ☐ Yeasty
- ☐ Malty
- ☐ Wheat
- ☐ Spicy

- ☐ Weak
- ☐ Strong
- ☐ Full-bodied
- ☐ Watery
- ☐ Clean
- ☐ Balanced

- ☐ Clear
- ☐ Cloudy
- ☐ Light
- ☐ Dark
- ☐ Flat
- ☐ Fizzy

- ☐ Fruity
- ☐ Citrus
- ☐ Floral
- ☐ Chocolate
- ☐ Toffee
- ☐ Coffee

TASTING NOTES

Name:

Brewery:

Country of origin:

Style:

Where sampled:

Hops:

ABV:

IBU/bitterness:

SRM/color:

Notes

Flavor profile:

- ☐ Sweet
- ☐ Sour
- ☐ Acidic
- ☐ Cask
- ☐ Keg
- ☐ Bottle

- ☐ Hoppy
- ☐ Bitter
- ☐ Yeasty
- ☐ Malty
- ☐ Wheat
- ☐ Spicy

- ☐ Weak
- ☐ Strong
- ☐ Full-bodied
- ☐ Watery
- ☐ Clean
- ☐ Balanced

- ☐ Clear
- ☐ Cloudy
- ☐ Light
- ☐ Dark
- ☐ Flat
- ☐ Fizzy

- ☐ Fruity
- ☐ Citrus
- ☐ Floral
- ☐ Chocolate
- ☐ Toffee
- ☐ Coffee

TASTING NOTES

Name:

Brewery:

Country of origin:

Style:

Where sampled:

Hops:

ABV:

IBU/bitterness:

SRM/color:

Notes

Flavor profile:

☐ Sweet	☐ Hoppy	☐ Weak	☐ Clear	☐ Fruity
☐ Sour	☐ Bitter	☐ Strong	☐ Cloudy	☐ Citrus
☐ Acidic	☐ Yeasty	☐ Full-bodied	☐ Light	☐ Floral
☐ Cask	☐ Malty	☐ Watery	☐ Dark	☐ Chocolate
☐ Keg	☐ Wheat	☐ Clean	☐ Flat	☐ Toffee
☐ Bottle	☐ Spicy	☐ Balanced	☐ Fizzy	☐ Coffee

TASTING NOTES

Name:

Brewery:

Country of origin:

Style:

Where sampled:

Hops:

ABV:

IBU/bitterness:

SRM/color:

Notes

Flavor profile:

☐ Sweet	☐ Hoppy	☐ Weak	☐ Clear	☐ Fruity
☐ Sour	☐ Bitter	☐ Strong	☐ Cloudy	☐ Citrus
☐ Acidic	☐ Yeasty	☐ Full-bodied	☐ Light	☐ Floral
☐ Cask	☐ Malty	☐ Watery	☐ Dark	☐ Chocolate
☐ Keg	☐ Wheat	☐ Clean	☐ Flat	☐ Toffee
☐ Bottle	☐ Spicy	☐ Balanced	☐ Fizzy	☐ Coffee

TASTING NOTES

Name:

Brewery:

Country of origin:

Style:

Where sampled:

Hops:

ABV:

IBU/bitterness:

SRM/color:

Notes

Flavor profile:

- [ ] Sweet
- [ ] Sour
- [ ] Acidic
- [ ] Cask
- [ ] Keg
- [ ] Bottle

- [ ] Hoppy
- [ ] Bitter
- [ ] Yeasty
- [ ] Malty
- [ ] Wheat
- [ ] Spicy

- [ ] Weak
- [ ] Strong
- [ ] Full-bodied
- [ ] Watery
- [ ] Clean
- [ ] Balanced

- [ ] Clear
- [ ] Cloudy
- [ ] Light
- [ ] Dark
- [ ] Flat
- [ ] Fizzy

- [ ] Fruity
- [ ] Citrus
- [ ] Floral
- [ ] Chocolate
- [ ] Toffee
- [ ] Coffee

TASTING NOTES

Name:

Brewery:

Country of origin:

Style:

Where sampled:

Hops:

ABV:

IBU/bitterness:

SRM/color:

Notes

Flavor profile:

- ☐ Sweet
- ☐ Sour
- ☐ Acidic
- ☐ Cask
- ☐ Keg
- ☐ Bottle

- ☐ Hoppy
- ☐ Bitter
- ☐ Yeasty
- ☐ Malty
- ☐ Wheat
- ☐ Spicy

- ☐ Weak
- ☐ Strong
- ☐ Full-bodied
- ☐ Watery
- ☐ Clean
- ☐ Balanced

- ☐ Clear
- ☐ Cloudy
- ☐ Light
- ☐ Dark
- ☐ Flat
- ☐ Fizzy

- ☐ Fruity
- ☐ Citrus
- ☐ Floral
- ☐ Chocolate
- ☐ Toffee
- ☐ Coffee

TASTING NOTES

Name:

Brewery:

Country of origin:

Style:

Where sampled:

Hops:

ABV:

IBU/bitterness:

SRM/color:

Notes

Flavor profile:

☐ Sweet	☐ Hoppy	☐ Weak	☐ Clear	☐ Fruity
☐ Sour	☐ Bitter	☐ Strong	☐ Cloudy	☐ Citrus
☐ Acidic	☐ Yeasty	☐ Full-bodied	☐ Light	☐ Floral
☐ Cask	☐ Malty	☐ Watery	☐ Dark	☐ Chocolate
☐ Keg	☐ Wheat	☐ Clean	☐ Flat	☐ Toffee
☐ Bottle	☐ Spicy	☐ Balanced	☐ Fizzy	☐ Coffee

TASTING NOTES

Name:

Brewery:

Country of origin:

Style:

Where sampled:

Hops:

ABV:

IBU/bitterness:

SRM/color:

Notes

Flavor profile:

☐ Sweet	☐ Hoppy	☐ Weak	☐ Clear	☐ Fruity
☐ Sour	☐ Bitter	☐ Strong	☐ Cloudy	☐ Citrus
☐ Acidic	☐ Yeasty	☐ Full-bodied	☐ Light	☐ Floral
☐ Cask	☐ Malty	☐ Watery	☐ Dark	☐ Chocolate
☐ Keg	☐ Wheat	☐ Clean	☐ Flat	☐ Toffee
☐ Bottle	☐ Spicy	☐ Balanced	☐ Fizzy	☐ Coffee

TASTING NOTES

Name:

Brewery:

Country of origin:

Style:

Where sampled:

Hops:

ABV:

IBU/bitterness:

SRM/color:

Notes:

Flavor profile:

☐ Sweet	☐ Hoppy	☐ Weak	☐ Clear	☐ Fruity
☐ Sour	☐ Bitter	☐ Strong	☐ Cloudy	☐ Citrus
☐ Acidic	☐ Yeasty	☐ Full-bodied	☐ Light	☐ Floral
☐ Cask	☐ Malty	☐ Watery	☐ Dark	☐ Chocolate
☐ Keg	☐ Wheat	☐ Clean	☐ Flat	☐ Toffee
☐ Bottle	☐ Spicy	☐ Balanced	☐ Fizzy	☐ Coffee

TASTING NOTES

Name:

Brewery:

Country of origin:

Style:

Where sampled:

Hops:

ABV:

IBU/bitterness:

SRM/color:

Notes:

Flavor profile:

- ☐ Sweet
- ☐ Sour
- ☐ Acidic
- ☐ Cask
- ☐ Keg
- ☐ Bottle

- ☐ Hoppy
- ☐ Bitter
- ☐ Yeasty
- ☐ Malty
- ☐ Wheat
- ☐ Spicy

- ☐ Weak
- ☐ Strong
- ☐ Full-bodied
- ☐ Watery
- ☐ Clean
- ☐ Balanced

- ☐ Clear
- ☐ Cloudy
- ☐ Light
- ☐ Dark
- ☐ Flat
- ☐ Fizzy

- ☐ Fruity
- ☐ Citrus
- ☐ Floral
- ☐ Chocolate
- ☐ Toffee
- ☐ Coffee

TASTING NOTES

Name:

Brewery:

Country of origin:

Style:

Where sampled:

Hops:

ABV:

IBU/bitterness:

SRM/color:

Notes:

Flavor profile:

- ☐ Sweet
- ☐ Sour
- ☐ Acidic
- ☐ Cask
- ☐ Keg
- ☐ Bottle

- ☐ Hoppy
- ☐ Bitter
- ☐ Yeasty
- ☐ Malty
- ☐ Wheat
- ☐ Spicy

- ☐ Weak
- ☐ Strong
- ☐ Full-bodied
- ☐ Watery
- ☐ Clean
- ☐ Balanced

- ☐ Clear
- ☐ Cloudy
- ☐ Light
- ☐ Dark
- ☐ Flat
- ☐ Fizzy

- ☐ Fruity
- ☐ Citrus
- ☐ Floral
- ☐ Chocolate
- ☐ Toffee
- ☐ Coffee

TASTING NOTES

Name:

Brewery:

Country of origin:

Style:

Where sampled:

Hops:

ABV:

IBU/bitterness:

SRM/color:

Notes:

Flavor profile:

- ☐ Sweet
- ☐ Sour
- ☐ Acidic
- ☐ Cask
- ☐ Keg
- ☐ Bottle

- ☐ Hoppy
- ☐ Bitter
- ☐ Yeasty
- ☐ Malty
- ☐ Wheat
- ☐ Spicy

- ☐ Weak
- ☐ Strong
- ☐ Full-bodied
- ☐ Watery
- ☐ Clean
- ☐ Balanced

- ☐ Clear
- ☐ Cloudy
- ☐ Light
- ☐ Dark
- ☐ Flat
- ☐ Fizzy

- ☐ Fruity
- ☐ Citrus
- ☐ Floral
- ☐ Chocolate
- ☐ Toffee
- ☐ Coffee

TASTING NOTES

Name:

Brewery:

Country of origin:

Style:

Where sampled:

Hops:

ABV:

IBU/bitterness:

SRM/color:

Notes:

Flavor profile:

- ☐ Sweet
- ☐ Sour
- ☐ Acidic
- ☐ Cask
- ☐ Keg
- ☐ Bottle

- ☐ Hoppy
- ☐ Bitter
- ☐ Yeasty
- ☐ Malty
- ☐ Wheat
- ☐ Spicy

- ☐ Weak
- ☐ Strong
- ☐ Full-bodied
- ☐ Watery
- ☐ Clean
- ☐ Balanced

- ☐ Clear
- ☐ Cloudy
- ☐ Light
- ☐ Dark
- ☐ Flat
- ☐ Fizzy

- ☐ Fruity
- ☐ Citrus
- ☐ Floral
- ☐ Chocolate
- ☐ Toffee
- ☐ Coffee

TASTING NOTES

Name:

Brewery:

Country of origin:

Style:

Where sampled:

Hops:

ABV:

IBU/bitterness:

SRM/color:

Notes:

Flavor profile:

☐ Sweet	☐ Hoppy	☐ Weak	☐ Clear	☐ Fruity
☐ Sour	☐ Bitter	☐ Strong	☐ Cloudy	☐ Citrus
☐ Acidic	☐ Yeasty	☐ Full-bodied	☐ Light	☐ Floral
☐ Cask	☐ Malty	☐ Watery	☐ Dark	☐ Chocolate
☐ Keg	☐ Wheat	☐ Clean	☐ Flat	☐ Toffee
☐ Bottle	☐ Spicy	☐ Balanced	☐ Fizzy	☐ Coffee

TASTING NOTES

Name:

Brewery:

Country of origin:

Style:

Where sampled:

Hops:

ABV:

IBU/bitterness:

SRM/color:

Notes:

Flavor profile:

☐ Sweet	☐ Hoppy	☐ Weak	☐ Clear	☐ Fruity
☐ Sour	☐ Bitter	☐ Strong	☐ Cloudy	☐ Citrus
☐ Acidic	☐ Yeasty	☐ Full-bodied	☐ Light	☐ Floral
☐ Cask	☐ Malty	☐ Watery	☐ Dark	☐ Chocolate
☐ Keg	☐ Wheat	☐ Clean	☐ Flat	☐ Toffee
☐ Bottle	☐ Spicy	☐ Balanced	☐ Fizzy	☐ Coffee

TASTING NOTES

Name: ....

Brewery: ....

Country of origin: ....

Style: ....

Where sampled: ....

Hops: ....

ABV: ....

IBU/bitterness: ....

SRM/color: ....

Notes: ....

....

....

Flavor profile:

☐ Sweet	☐ Hoppy	☐ Weak	☐ Clear	☐ Fruity
☐ Sour	☐ Bitter	☐ Strong	☐ Cloudy	☐ Citrus
☐ Acidic	☐ Yeasty	☐ Full-bodied	☐ Light	☐ Floral
☐ Cask	☐ Malty	☐ Watery	☐ Dark	☐ Chocolate
☐ Keg	☐ Wheat	☐ Clean	☐ Flat	☐ Toffee
☐ Bottle	☐ Spicy	☐ Balanced	☐ Fizzy	☐ Coffee

TASTING NOTES

Name:

Brewery:

Country of origin:

Style:

Where sampled:

Hops:

ABV:

IBU/bitterness:

SRM/color:

Notes:

Flavor profile:

☐ Sweet	☐ Hoppy	☐ Weak	☐ Clear	☐ Fruity
☐ Sour	☐ Bitter	☐ Strong	☐ Cloudy	☐ Citrus
☐ Acidic	☐ Yeasty	☐ Full-bodied	☐ Light	☐ Floral
☐ Cask	☐ Malty	☐ Watery	☐ Dark	☐ Chocolate
☐ Keg	☐ Wheat	☐ Clean	☐ Flat	☐ Toffee
☐ Bottle	☐ Spicy	☐ Balanced	☐ Fizzy	☐ Coffee

TASTING NOTES

Name:

Brewery:

Country of origin:

Style:

Where sampled:

Hops:

ABV:

IBU/bitterness:

SRM/color:

Notes:

Flavor profile:

- ☐ Sweet
- ☐ Sour
- ☐ Acidic
- ☐ Cask
- ☐ Keg
- ☐ Bottle

- ☐ Hoppy
- ☐ Bitter
- ☐ Yeasty
- ☐ Malty
- ☐ Wheat
- ☐ Spicy

- ☐ Weak
- ☐ Strong
- ☐ Full-bodied
- ☐ Watery
- ☐ Clean
- ☐ Balanced

- ☐ Clear
- ☐ Cloudy
- ☐ Light
- ☐ Dark
- ☐ Flat
- ☐ Fizzy

- ☐ Fruity
- ☐ Citrus
- ☐ Floral
- ☐ Chocolate
- ☐ Toffee
- ☐ Coffee

TASTING NOTES

Name:

Brewery:

Country of origin:

Style:

Where sampled:

Hops:

ABV:

IBU/bitterness:

SRM/color:

Notes:

Flavor profile:

☐ Sweet	☐ Hoppy	☐ Weak	☐ Clear	☐ Fruity
☐ Sour	☐ Bitter	☐ Strong	☐ Cloudy	☐ Citrus
☐ Acidic	☐ Yeasty	☐ Full-bodied	☐ Light	☐ Floral
☐ Cask	☐ Malty	☐ Watery	☐ Dark	☐ Chocolate
☐ Keg	☐ Wheat	☐ Clean	☐ Flat	☐ Toffee
☐ Bottle	☐ Spicy	☐ Balanced	☐ Fizzy	☐ Coffee

TASTING NOTES

Name:

Brewery:

Country of origin:

Style:

Where sampled:

Hops:

ABV:

IBU/bitterness:

SRM/color:

Notes:

Flavor profile:

☐ Sweet	☐ Hoppy	☐ Weak	☐ Clear	☐ Fruity
☐ Sour	☐ Bitter	☐ Strong	☐ Cloudy	☐ Citrus
☐ Acidic	☐ Yeasty	☐ Full-bodied	☐ Light	☐ Floral
☐ Cask	☐ Malty	☐ Watery	☐ Dark	☐ Chocolate
☐ Keg	☐ Wheat	☐ Clean	☐ Flat	☐ Toffee
☐ Bottle	☐ Spicy	☐ Balanced	☐ Fizzy	☐ Coffee

TASTING NOTES

Name:

Brewery:

Country of origin:

Style:

Where sampled:

Hops:

ABV:

IBU/bitterness:

SRM/color:

Notes:

Flavor profile:

- Sweet
- Sour
- Acidic
- Cask
- Keg
- Bottle

- Hoppy
- Bitter
- Yeasty
- Malty
- Wheat
- Spicy

- Weak
- Strong
- Full-bodied
- Watery
- Clean
- Balanced

- Clear
- Cloudy
- Light
- Dark
- Flat
- Fizzy

- Fruity
- Citrus
- Floral
- Chocolate
- Toffee
- Coffee

TASTING NOTES

Name:

Brewery:

Country of origin:

Style:

Where sampled:

Hops:

ABV:

IBU/bitterness:

SRM/color:

Notes:

Flavor profile:

- ☐ Sweet
- ☐ Sour
- ☐ Acidic
- ☐ Cask
- ☐ Keg
- ☐ Bottle

- ☐ Hoppy
- ☐ Bitter
- ☐ Yeasty
- ☐ Malty
- ☐ Wheat
- ☐ Spicy

- ☐ Weak
- ☐ Strong
- ☐ Full-bodied
- ☐ Watery
- ☐ Clean
- ☐ Balanced

- ☐ Clear
- ☐ Cloudy
- ☐ Light
- ☐ Dark
- ☐ Flat
- ☐ Fizzy

- ☐ Fruity
- ☐ Citrus
- ☐ Floral
- ☐ Chocolate
- ☐ Toffee
- ☐ Coffee

TASTING NOTES

Name:

Brewery:

Country of origin:

Style:

Where sampled:

Hops:

ABV:

IBU/bitterness:

SRM/color:

Notes:

Flavor profile:

☐ Sweet	☐ Hoppy	☐ Weak	☐ Clear	☐ Fruity
☐ Sour	☐ Bitter	☐ Strong	☐ Cloudy	☐ Citrus
☐ Acidic	☐ Yeasty	☐ Full-bodied	☐ Light	☐ Floral
☐ Cask	☐ Malty	☐ Watery	☐ Dark	☐ Chocolate
☐ Keg	☐ Wheat	☐ Clean	☐ Flat	☐ Toffee
☐ Bottle	☐ Spicy	☐ Balanced	☐ Fizzy	☐ Coffee

TASTING NOTES

Name:

Brewery:

Country of origin:

Style:

Where sampled:

Hops:

ABV:

IBU/bitterness:

SRM/color:

Notes:

Flavor profile:

- ☐ Sweet
- ☐ Sour
- ☐ Acidic
- ☐ Cask
- ☐ Keg
- ☐ Bottle

- ☐ Hoppy
- ☐ Bitter
- ☐ Yeasty
- ☐ Malty
- ☐ Wheat
- ☐ Spicy

- ☐ Weak
- ☐ Strong
- ☐ Full-bodied
- ☐ Watery
- ☐ Clean
- ☐ Balanced

- ☐ Clear
- ☐ Cloudy
- ☐ Light
- ☐ Dark
- ☐ Flat
- ☐ Fizzy

- ☐ Fruity
- ☐ Citrus
- ☐ Floral
- ☐ Chocolate
- ☐ Toffee
- ☐ Coffee

TASTING NOTES

Name:

Brewery:

Country of origin:

Style:

Where sampled:

Hops:

ABV:

IBU/bitterness:

SRM/color:

Notes:

Flavor profile:

- ☐ Sweet
- ☐ Sour
- ☐ Acidic
- ☐ Cask
- ☐ Keg
- ☐ Bottle

- ☐ Hoppy
- ☐ Bitter
- ☐ Yeasty
- ☐ Malty
- ☐ Wheat
- ☐ Spicy

- ☐ Weak
- ☐ Strong
- ☐ Full-bodied
- ☐ Watery
- ☐ Clean
- ☐ Balanced

- ☐ Clear
- ☐ Cloudy
- ☐ Light
- ☐ Dark
- ☐ Flat
- ☐ Fizzy

- ☐ Fruity
- ☐ Citrus
- ☐ Floral
- ☐ Chocolate
- ☐ Toffee
- ☐ Coffee

TASTING NOTES

Name:

Brewery:

Country of origin:

Style:

Where sampled:

Hops:

ABV:

IBU/bitterness:

SRM/color:

Notes:

Flavor profile:

☐ Sweet	☐ Hoppy	☐ Weak	☐ Clear	☐ Fruity
☐ Sour	☐ Bitter	☐ Strong	☐ Cloudy	☐ Citrus
☐ Acidic	☐ Yeasty	☐ Full-bodied	☐ Light	☐ Floral
☐ Cask	☐ Malty	☐ Watery	☐ Dark	☐ Chocolate
☐ Keg	☐ Wheat	☐ Clean	☐ Flat	☐ Toffee
☐ Bottle	☐ Spicy	☐ Balanced	☐ Fizzy	☐ Coffee

TASTING NOTES

Name:

Brewery:

Country of origin:

Style:

Where sampled:

Hops:

ABV:

IBU/bitterness:

SRM/color:

Notes:

Flavor profile:

- ☐ Sweet
- ☐ Sour
- ☐ Acidic
- ☐ Cask
- ☐ Keg
- ☐ Bottle

- ☐ Hoppy
- ☐ Bitter
- ☐ Yeasty
- ☐ Malty
- ☐ Wheat
- ☐ Spicy

- ☐ Weak
- ☐ Strong
- ☐ Full-bodied
- ☐ Watery
- ☐ Clean
- ☐ Balanced

- ☐ Clear
- ☐ Cloudy
- ☐ Light
- ☐ Dark
- ☐ Flat
- ☐ Fizzy

- ☐ Fruity
- ☐ Citrus
- ☐ Floral
- ☐ Chocolate
- ☐ Toffee
- ☐ Coffee

TASTING NOTES

Name:

Brewery:

Country of origin:

Style:

Where sampled:

Hops:

ABV:

IBU/bitterness:

SRM/color:

Notes:

Flavor profile:

- ☐ Sweet
- ☐ Sour
- ☐ Acidic
- ☐ Cask
- ☐ Keg
- ☐ Bottle

- ☐ Hoppy
- ☐ Bitter
- ☐ Yeasty
- ☐ Malty
- ☐ Wheat
- ☐ Spicy

- ☐ Weak
- ☐ Strong
- ☐ Full-bodied
- ☐ Watery
- ☐ Clean
- ☐ Balanced

- ☐ Clear
- ☐ Cloudy
- ☐ Light
- ☐ Dark
- ☐ Flat
- ☐ Fizzy

- ☐ Fruity
- ☐ Citrus
- ☐ Floral
- ☐ Chocolate
- ☐ Toffee
- ☐ Coffee

TASTING NOTES

Name:

Brewery:

Country of origin:

Style:

Where sampled:

Hops:

ABV:

IBU/bitterness:

SRM/color:

Notes:

Flavor profile:

☐ Sweet	☐ Hoppy	☐ Weak	☐ Clear	☐ Fruity
☐ Sour	☐ Bitter	☐ Strong	☐ Cloudy	☐ Citrus
☐ Acidic	☐ Yeasty	☐ Full-bodied	☐ Light	☐ Floral
☐ Cask	☐ Malty	☐ Watery	☐ Dark	☐ Chocolate
☐ Keg	☐ Wheat	☐ Clean	☐ Flat	☐ Toffee
☐ Bottle	☐ Spicy	☐ Balanced	☐ Fizzy	☐ Coffee

TASTING NOTES

Name:

Brewery:

Country of origin:

Style:

Where sampled:

Hops:

ABV:

IBU/bitterness:

SRM/color:

Notes:

Flavor profile:

- ☐ Sweet
- ☐ Sour
- ☐ Acidic
- ☐ Cask
- ☐ Keg
- ☐ Bottle

- ☐ Hoppy
- ☐ Bitter
- ☐ Yeasty
- ☐ Malty
- ☐ Wheat
- ☐ Spicy

- ☐ Weak
- ☐ Strong
- ☐ Full-bodied
- ☐ Watery
- ☐ Clean
- ☐ Balanced

- ☐ Clear
- ☐ Cloudy
- ☐ Light
- ☐ Dark
- ☐ Flat
- ☐ Fizzy

- ☐ Fruity
- ☐ Citrus
- ☐ Floral
- ☐ Chocolate
- ☐ Toffee
- ☐ Coffee

TASTING NOTES

Name:

Brewery:

Country of origin:

Style:

Where sampled:

Hops:

ABV:

IBU/bitterness:

SRM/color:

Notes:

Flavor profile:

- ☐ Sweet
- ☐ Sour
- ☐ Acidic
- ☐ Cask
- ☐ Keg
- ☐ Bottle

- ☐ Hoppy
- ☐ Bitter
- ☐ Yeasty
- ☐ Malty
- ☐ Wheat
- ☐ Spicy

- ☐ Weak
- ☐ Strong
- ☐ Full-bodied
- ☐ Watery
- ☐ Clean
- ☐ Balanced

- ☐ Clear
- ☐ Cloudy
- ☐ Light
- ☐ Dark
- ☐ Flat
- ☐ Fizzy

- ☐ Fruity
- ☐ Citrus
- ☐ Floral
- ☐ Chocolate
- ☐ Toffee
- ☐ Coffee

TASTING NOTES

Name:

Brewery:

Country of origin:

Style:

Where sampled:

Hops:

ABV:

IBU/bitterness:

SRM/color:

Notes:

Flavor profile:

☐ Sweet	☐ Hoppy	☐ Weak	☐ Clear	☐ Fruity
☐ Sour	☐ Bitter	☐ Strong	☐ Cloudy	☐ Citrus
☐ Acidic	☐ Yeasty	☐ Full-bodied	☐ Light	☐ Floral
☐ Cask	☐ Malty	☐ Watery	☐ Dark	☐ Chocolate
☐ Keg	☐ Wheat	☐ Clean	☐ Flat	☐ Toffee
☐ Bottle	☐ Spicy	☐ Balanced	☐ Fizzy	☐ Coffee

TASTING NOTES

Name:

Brewery:

Country of origin:

Style:

Where sampled:

Hops:

ABV:

IBU/bitterness:

SRM/color:

Notes:

Flavor profile:

- ☐ Sweet
- ☐ Sour
- ☐ Acidic
- ☐ Cask
- ☐ Keg
- ☐ Bottle

- ☐ Hoppy
- ☐ Bitter
- ☐ Yeasty
- ☐ Malty
- ☐ Wheat
- ☐ Spicy

- ☐ Weak
- ☐ Strong
- ☐ Full-bodied
- ☐ Watery
- ☐ Clean
- ☐ Balanced

- ☐ Clear
- ☐ Cloudy
- ☐ Light
- ☐ Dark
- ☐ Flat
- ☐ Fizzy

- ☐ Fruity
- ☐ Citrus
- ☐ Floral
- ☐ Chocolate
- ☐ Toffee
- ☐ Coffee

TASTING NOTES

Name:

Brewery:

Country of origin:

Style:

Where sampled:

Hops:

ABV:

IBU/bitterness:

SRM/color:

Notes:

Flavor profile:

- ☐ Sweet
- ☐ Sour
- ☐ Acidic
- ☐ Cask
- ☐ Keg
- ☐ Bottle

- ☐ Hoppy
- ☐ Bitter
- ☐ Yeasty
- ☐ Malty
- ☐ Wheat
- ☐ Spicy

- ☐ Weak
- ☐ Strong
- ☐ Full-bodied
- ☐ Watery
- ☐ Clean
- ☐ Balanced

- ☐ Clear
- ☐ Cloudy
- ☐ Light
- ☐ Dark
- ☐ Flat
- ☐ Fizzy

- ☐ Fruity
- ☐ Citrus
- ☐ Floral
- ☐ Chocolate
- ☐ Toffee
- ☐ Coffee

TASTING NOTES

Name:

Brewery:

Country of origin:

Style:

Where sampled:

Hops:

ABV:

IBU/bitterness:

SRM/color:

Notes:

Flavor profile:

▢ Sweet	▢ Hoppy	▢ Weak	▢ Clear	▢ Fruity
▢ Sour	▢ Bitter	▢ Strong	▢ Cloudy	▢ Citrus
▢ Acidic	▢ Yeasty	▢ Full-bodied	▢ Light	▢ Floral
▢ Cask	▢ Malty	▢ Watery	▢ Dark	▢ Chocolate
▢ Keg	▢ Wheat	▢ Clean	▢ Flat	▢ Toffee
▢ Bottle	▢ Spicy	▢ Balanced	▢ Fizzy	▢ Coffee

TASTING NOTES

Name:

Brewery:

Country of origin:

Style:

Where sampled:

Hops:

ABV:

IBU/bitterness:

SRM/color:

Notes:

Flavor profile:

☐ Sweet	☐ Hoppy	☐ Weak	☐ Clear	☐ Fruity
☐ Sour	☐ Bitter	☐ Strong	☐ Cloudy	☐ Citrus
☐ Acidic	☐ Yeasty	☐ Full-bodied	☐ Light	☐ Floral
☐ Cask	☐ Malty	☐ Watery	☐ Dark	☐ Chocolate
☐ Keg	☐ Wheat	☐ Clean	☐ Flat	☐ Toffee
☐ Bottle	☐ Spicy	☐ Balanced	☐ Fizzy	☐ Coffee

TASTING NOTES

Name:

Brewery:

Country of origin:

Style:

Where sampled:

Hops:

ABV:

IBU/bitterness:

SRM/color:

Notes:

Flavor profile:

- ☐ Sweet
- ☐ Sour
- ☐ Acidic
- ☐ Cask
- ☐ Keg
- ☐ Bottle

- ☐ Hoppy
- ☐ Bitter
- ☐ Yeasty
- ☐ Malty
- ☐ Wheat
- ☐ Spicy

- ☐ Weak
- ☐ Strong
- ☐ Full-bodied
- ☐ Watery
- ☐ Clean
- ☐ Balanced

- ☐ Clear
- ☐ Cloudy
- ☐ Light
- ☐ Dark
- ☐ Flat
- ☐ Fizzy

- ☐ Fruity
- ☐ Citrus
- ☐ Floral
- ☐ Chocolate
- ☐ Toffee
- ☐ Coffee

TASTING NOTES

Name:

Brewery:

Country of origin:

Style:

Where sampled:

Hops:

ABV:

IBU/bitterness:

SRM/color:

Notes:

Flavor profile:

☐ Sweet	☐ Hoppy	☐ Weak	☐ Clear	☐ Fruity
☐ Sour	☐ Bitter	☐ Strong	☐ Cloudy	☐ Citrus
☐ Acidic	☐ Yeasty	☐ Full-bodied	☐ Light	☐ Floral
☐ Cask	☐ Malty	☐ Watery	☐ Dark	☐ Chocolate
☐ Keg	☐ Wheat	☐ Clean	☐ Flat	☐ Toffee
☐ Bottle	☐ Spicy	☐ Balanced	☐ Fizzy	☐ Coffee

TASTING NOTES

Name:

Brewery:

Country of origin:

Style:

Where sampled:

Hops:

ABV:

IBU/bitterness:

SRM/color:

Notes:

Flavor profile:

☐ Sweet	☐ Hoppy	☐ Weak	☐ Clear	☐ Fruity
☐ Sour	☐ Bitter	☐ Strong	☐ Cloudy	☐ Citrus
☐ Acidic	☐ Yeasty	☐ Full-bodied	☐ Light	☐ Floral
☐ Cask	☐ Malty	☐ Watery	☐ Dark	☐ Chocolate
☐ Keg	☐ Wheat	☐ Clean	☐ Flat	☐ Toffee
☐ Bottle	☐ Spicy	☐ Balanced	☐ Fizzy	☐ Coffee

TASTING NOTES

Name:

Brewery:

Country of origin:

Style:

Where sampled:

Hops:

ABV:

IBU/bitterness:

SRM/color:

Notes:

Flavor profile:

- ☐ Sweet
- ☐ Sour
- ☐ Acidic
- ☐ Cask
- ☐ Keg
- ☐ Bottle

- ☐ Hoppy
- ☐ Bitter
- ☐ Yeasty
- ☐ Malty
- ☐ Wheat
- ☐ Spicy

- ☐ Weak
- ☐ Strong
- ☐ Full-bodied
- ☐ Watery
- ☐ Clean
- ☐ Balanced

- ☐ Clear
- ☐ Cloudy
- ☐ Light
- ☐ Dark
- ☐ Flat
- ☐ Fizzy

- ☐ Fruity
- ☐ Citrus
- ☐ Floral
- ☐ Chocolate
- ☐ Toffee
- ☐ Coffee

TASTING NOTES

Name:

Brewery:

Country of origin:

Style:

Where sampled:

Hops:

ABV:

IBU/bitterness:

SRM/color:

Notes:

Flavor profile:

- ☐ Sweet
- ☐ Sour
- ☐ Acidic
- ☐ Cask
- ☐ Keg
- ☐ Bottle

- ☐ Hoppy
- ☐ Bitter
- ☐ Yeasty
- ☐ Malty
- ☐ Wheat
- ☐ Spicy

- ☐ Weak
- ☐ Strong
- ☐ Full-bodied
- ☐ Watery
- ☐ Clean
- ☐ Balanced

- ☐ Clear
- ☐ Cloudy
- ☐ Light
- ☐ Dark
- ☐ Flat
- ☐ Fizzy

- ☐ Fruity
- ☐ Citrus
- ☐ Floral
- ☐ Chocolate
- ☐ Toffee
- ☐ Coffee

TASTING NOTES

Name:

Brewery:

Country of origin:

Style:

Where sampled:

Hops:

ABV:

IBU/bitterness:

SRM/color:

Notes:

Flavor profile:

☐ Sweet	☐ Hoppy	☐ Weak	☐ Clear	☐ Fruity
☐ Sour	☐ Bitter	☐ Strong	☐ Cloudy	☐ Citrus
☐ Acidic	☐ Yeasty	☐ Full-bodied	☐ Light	☐ Floral
☐ Cask	☐ Malty	☐ Watery	☐ Dark	☐ Chocolate
☐ Keg	☐ Wheat	☐ Clean	☐ Flat	☐ Toffee
☐ Bottle	☐ Spicy	☐ Balanced	☐ Fizzy	☐ Coffee

TASTING NOTES

Name:

Brewery:

Country of origin:

Style:

Where sampled:

Hops:

ABV:

IBU/bitterness:

SRM/color:

Notes:

Flavor profile:

☐ Sweet	☐ Hoppy	☐ Weak	☐ Clear	☐ Fruity
☐ Sour	☐ Bitter	☐ Strong	☐ Cloudy	☐ Citrus
☐ Acidic	☐ Yeasty	☐ Full-bodied	☐ Light	☐ Floral
☐ Cask	☐ Malty	☐ Watery	☐ Dark	☐ Chocolate
☐ Keg	☐ Wheat	☐ Clean	☐ Flat	☐ Toffee
☐ Bottle	☐ Spicy	☐ Balanced	☐ Fizzy	☐ Coffee

TASTING NOTES

Name:

Brewery:

Country of origin:

Style:

Where sampled:

Hops:

ABV:

IBU/bitterness:

SRM/color:

Notes:

Flavor profile:

☐ Sweet	☐ Hoppy	☐ Weak	☐ Clear	☐ Fruity
☐ Sour	☐ Bitter	☐ Strong	☐ Cloudy	☐ Citrus
☐ Acidic	☐ Yeasty	☐ Full-bodied	☐ Light	☐ Floral
☐ Cask	☐ Malty	☐ Watery	☐ Dark	☐ Chocolate
☐ Keg	☐ Wheat	☐ Clean	☐ Flat	☐ Toffee
☐ Bottle	☐ Spicy	☐ Balanced	☐ Fizzy	☐ Coffee

TASTING NOTES

Name:

Brewery:

Country of origin:

Style:

Where sampled:

Hops:

ABV:

IBU/bitterness:

SRM/color:

Notes:

Flavor profile:

☐ Sweet	☐ Hoppy	☐ Weak	☐ Clear	☐ Fruity
☐ Sour	☐ Bitter	☐ Strong	☐ Cloudy	☐ Citrus
☐ Acidic	☐ Yeasty	☐ Full-bodied	☐ Light	☐ Floral
☐ Cask	☐ Malty	☐ Watery	☐ Dark	☐ Chocolate
☐ Keg	☐ Wheat	☐ Clean	☐ Flat	☐ Toffee
☐ Bottle	☐ Spicy	☐ Balanced	☐ Fizzy	☐ Coffee

TASTING NOTES

Name:

Brewery:

Country of origin:

Style:

Where sampled:

Hops:

ABV:

IBU/bitterness:

SRM/color:

Notes:

Flavor profile:

- ☐ Sweet
- ☐ Sour
- ☐ Acidic
- ☐ Cask
- ☐ Keg
- ☐ Bottle

- ☐ Hoppy
- ☐ Bitter
- ☐ Yeasty
- ☐ Malty
- ☐ Wheat
- ☐ Spicy

- ☐ Weak
- ☐ Strong
- ☐ Full-bodied
- ☐ Watery
- ☐ Clean
- ☐ Balanced

- ☐ Clear
- ☐ Cloudy
- ☐ Light
- ☐ Dark
- ☐ Flat
- ☐ Fizzy

- ☐ Fruity
- ☐ Citrus
- ☐ Floral
- ☐ Chocolate
- ☐ Toffee
- ☐ Coffee

TASTING NOTES

Name:

Brewery:

Country of origin:

Style:

Where sampled:

Hops:

ABV:

IBU/bitterness:

SRM/color:

Notes:

Flavor profile:

☐ Sweet	☐ Hoppy	☐ Weak	☐ Clear	☐ Fruity
☐ Sour	☐ Bitter	☐ Strong	☐ Cloudy	☐ Citrus
☐ Acidic	☐ Yeasty	☐ Full-bodied	☐ Light	☐ Floral
☐ Cask	☐ Malty	☐ Watery	☐ Dark	☐ Chocolate
☐ Keg	☐ Wheat	☐ Clean	☐ Flat	☐ Toffee
☐ Bottle	☐ Spicy	☐ Balanced	☐ Fizzy	☐ Coffee

TASTING NOTES

Name:

Brewery:

Country of origin:

Style:

Where sampled:

Hops:

ABV:

IBU/bitterness:

SRM/color:

Notes:

Flavor profile:

- ☐ Sweet
- ☐ Sour
- ☐ Acidic
- ☐ Cask
- ☐ Keg
- ☐ Bottle

- ☐ Hoppy
- ☐ Bitter
- ☐ Yeasty
- ☐ Malty
- ☐ Wheat
- ☐ Spicy

- ☐ Weak
- ☐ Strong
- ☐ Full-bodied
- ☐ Watery
- ☐ Clean
- ☐ Balanced

- ☐ Clear
- ☐ Cloudy
- ☐ Light
- ☐ Dark
- ☐ Flat
- ☐ Fizzy

- ☐ Fruity
- ☐ Citrus
- ☐ Floral
- ☐ Chocolate
- ☐ Toffee
- ☐ Coffee

TASTING NOTES

Name:

Brewery:

Country of origin:

Style:

Where sampled:

Hops:

ABV:

IBU/bitterness:

SRM/color:

Notes:

Flavor profile:

- ☐ Sweet
- ☐ Sour
- ☐ Acidic
- ☐ Cask
- ☐ Keg
- ☐ Bottle

- ☐ Hoppy
- ☐ Bitter
- ☐ Yeasty
- ☐ Malty
- ☐ Wheat
- ☐ Spicy

- ☐ Weak
- ☐ Strong
- ☐ Full-bodied
- ☐ Watery
- ☐ Clean
- ☐ Balanced

- ☐ Clear
- ☐ Cloudy
- ☐ Light
- ☐ Dark
- ☐ Flat
- ☐ Fizzy

- ☐ Fruity
- ☐ Citrus
- ☐ Floral
- ☐ Chocolate
- ☐ Toffee
- ☐ Coffee

TASTING NOTES

Name:

Brewery:

Country of origin:

Style:

Where sampled:

Hops:

ABV:

IBU/bitterness:

SRM/color:

Notes:

Flavor profile:

☐ Sweet	☐ Hoppy	☐ Weak	☐ Clear	☐ Fruity
☐ Sour	☐ Bitter	☐ Strong	☐ Cloudy	☐ Citrus
☐ Acidic	☐ Yeasty	☐ Full-bodied	☐ Light	☐ Floral
☐ Cask	☐ Malty	☐ Watery	☐ Dark	☐ Chocolate
☐ Keg	☐ Wheat	☐ Clean	☐ Flat	☐ Toffee
☐ Bottle	☐ Spicy	☐ Balanced	☐ Fizzy	☐ Coffee

TASTING NOTES

Name:

Brewery:

Country of origin:

Style:

Where sampled:

Hops:

ABV:

IBU/bitterness:

SRM/color:

Notes:

Flavor profile:

☐ Sweet	☐ Hoppy	☐ Weak	☐ Clear	☐ Fruity
☐ Sour	☐ Bitter	☐ Strong	☐ Cloudy	☐ Citrus
☐ Acidic	☐ Yeasty	☐ Full-bodied	☐ Light	☐ Floral
☐ Cask	☐ Malty	☐ Watery	☐ Dark	☐ Chocolate
☐ Keg	☐ Wheat	☐ Clean	☐ Flat	☐ Toffee
☐ Bottle	☐ Spicy	☐ Balanced	☐ Fizzy	☐ Coffee

TASTING NOTES

Name:

Brewery:

Country of origin:

Style:

Where sampled:

Hops:

ABV:

IBU/bitterness:

SRM/color:

Notes:

Flavor profile:

- ☐ Sweet
- ☐ Sour
- ☐ Acidic
- ☐ Cask
- ☐ Keg
- ☐ Bottle

- ☐ Hoppy
- ☐ Bitter
- ☐ Yeasty
- ☐ Malty
- ☐ Wheat
- ☐ Spicy

- ☐ Weak
- ☐ Strong
- ☐ Full-bodied
- ☐ Watery
- ☐ Clean
- ☐ Balanced

- ☐ Clear
- ☐ Cloudy
- ☐ Light
- ☐ Dark
- ☐ Flat
- ☐ Fizzy

- ☐ Fruity
- ☐ Citrus
- ☐ Floral
- ☐ Chocolate
- ☐ Toffee
- ☐ Coffee

TASTING NOTES

Name:

Brewery:

Country of origin:

Style:

Where sampled:

Hops:

ABV:

IBU/bitterness:

SRM/color:

Notes:

Flavor profile:

☐ Sweet	☐ Hoppy	☐ Weak	☐ Clear	☐ Fruity
☐ Sour	☐ Bitter	☐ Strong	☐ Cloudy	☐ Citrus
☐ Acidic	☐ Yeasty	☐ Full-bodied	☐ Light	☐ Floral
☐ Cask	☐ Malty	☐ Watery	☐ Dark	☐ Chocolate
☐ Keg	☐ Wheat	☐ Clean	☐ Flat	☐ Toffee
☐ Bottle	☐ Spicy	☐ Balanced	☐ Fizzy	☐ Coffee

TASTING NOTES

Name:

Brewery:

Country of origin:

Style:

Where sampled:

Hops:

ABV:

IBU/bitterness:

SRM/color:

Notes:

Flavor profile:

- ☐ Sweet
- ☐ Sour
- ☐ Acidic
- ☐ Cask
- ☐ Keg
- ☐ Bottle

- ☐ Hoppy
- ☐ Bitter
- ☐ Yeasty
- ☐ Malty
- ☐ Wheat
- ☐ Spicy

- ☐ Weak
- ☐ Strong
- ☐ Full-bodied
- ☐ Watery
- ☐ Clean
- ☐ Balanced

- ☐ Clear
- ☐ Cloudy
- ☐ Light
- ☐ Dark
- ☐ Flat
- ☐ Fizzy

- ☐ Fruity
- ☐ Citrus
- ☐ Floral
- ☐ Chocolate
- ☐ Toffee
- ☐ Coffee

TASTING NOTES

Name:

Brewery:

Country of origin:

Style:

Where sampled:

Hops:

ABV:

IBU/bitterness:

SRM/color:

Notes:

Flavor profile:

☐ Sweet	☐ Hoppy	☐ Weak	☐ Clear	☐ Fruity
☐ Sour	☐ Bitter	☐ Strong	☐ Cloudy	☐ Citrus
☐ Acidic	☐ Yeasty	☐ Full-bodied	☐ Light	☐ Floral
☐ Cask	☐ Malty	☐ Watery	☐ Dark	☐ Chocolate
☐ Keg	☐ Wheat	☐ Clean	☐ Flat	☐ Toffee
☐ Bottle	☐ Spicy	☐ Balanced	☐ Fizzy	☐ Coffee

TASTING NOTES

Name:

Brewery:

Country of origin:

Style:

Where sampled:

Hops:

ABV:

IBU/bitterness:

SRM/color:

Notes:

Flavor profile:

- ☐ Sweet
- ☐ Sour
- ☐ Acidic
- ☐ Cask
- ☐ Keg
- ☐ Bottle

- ☐ Hoppy
- ☐ Bitter
- ☐ Yeasty
- ☐ Malty
- ☐ Wheat
- ☐ Spicy

- ☐ Weak
- ☐ Strong
- ☐ Full-bodied
- ☐ Watery
- ☐ Clean
- ☐ Balanced

- ☐ Clear
- ☐ Cloudy
- ☐ Light
- ☐ Dark
- ☐ Flat
- ☐ Fizzy

- ☐ Fruity
- ☐ Citrus
- ☐ Floral
- ☐ Chocolate
- ☐ Toffee
- ☐ Coffee

TASTING NOTES

Name:

Brewery:

Country of origin:

Style:

Where sampled:

Hops:

ABV:

IBU/bitterness:

SRM/color:

Notes:

Flavor profile:

- ☐ Sweet
- ☐ Sour
- ☐ Acidic
- ☐ Cask
- ☐ Keg
- ☐ Bottle

- ☐ Hoppy
- ☐ Bitter
- ☐ Yeasty
- ☐ Malty
- ☐ Wheat
- ☐ Spicy

- ☐ Weak
- ☐ Strong
- ☐ Full-bodied
- ☐ Watery
- ☐ Clean
- ☐ Balanced

- ☐ Clear
- ☐ Cloudy
- ☐ Light
- ☐ Dark
- ☐ Flat
- ☐ Fizzy

- ☐ Fruity
- ☐ Citrus
- ☐ Floral
- ☐ Chocolate
- ☐ Toffee
- ☐ Coffee

TASTING NOTES

Name:

Brewery:

Country of origin:

Style:

Where sampled:

Hops:

ABV:

IBU/bitterness:

SRM/color:

Notes:

Flavor profile:

☐ Sweet	☐ Hoppy	☐ Weak	☐ Clear	☐ Fruity
☐ Sour	☐ Bitter	☐ Strong	☐ Cloudy	☐ Citrus
☐ Acidic	☐ Yeasty	☐ Full-bodied	☐ Light	☐ Floral
☐ Cask	☐ Malty	☐ Watery	☐ Dark	☐ Chocolate
☐ Keg	☐ Wheat	☐ Clean	☐ Flat	☐ Toffee
☐ Bottle	☐ Spicy	☐ Balanced	☐ Fizzy	☐ Coffee

TASTING NOTES

Name:

Brewery:

Country of origin:

Style:

Where sampled:

Hops:

ABV:

IBU/bitterness:

SRM/color:

Notes:

Flavor profile:

▢ Sweet	▢ Hoppy	▢ Weak	▢ Clear	▢ Fruity
▢ Sour	▢ Bitter	▢ Strong	▢ Cloudy	▢ Citrus
▢ Acidic	▢ Yeasty	▢ Full-bodied	▢ Light	▢ Floral
▢ Cask	▢ Malty	▢ Watery	▢ Dark	▢ Chocolate
▢ Keg	▢ Wheat	▢ Clean	▢ Flat	▢ Toffee
▢ Bottle	▢ Spicy	▢ Balanced	▢ Fizzy	▢ Coffee

TASTING NOTES

Name:

Brewery:

Country of origin:

Style:

Where sampled:

Hops:

ABV:

IBU/bitterness:

SRM/color:

Notes:

Flavor profile:

☐ Sweet	☐ Hoppy	☐ Weak	☐ Clear	☐ Fruity
☐ Sour	☐ Bitter	☐ Strong	☐ Cloudy	☐ Citrus
☐ Acidic	☐ Yeasty	☐ Full-bodied	☐ Light	☐ Floral
☐ Cask	☐ Malty	☐ Watery	☐ Dark	☐ Chocolate
☐ Keg	☐ Wheat	☐ Clean	☐ Flat	☐ Toffee
☐ Bottle	☐ Spicy	☐ Balanced	☐ Fizzy	☐ Coffee

TASTING NOTES

Name:

Brewery:

Country of origin:

Style:

Where sampled:

Hops:

ABV:

IBU/bitterness:

SRM/color:

Notes:

Flavor profile:

☐ Sweet	☐ Hoppy	☐ Weak	☐ Clear	☐ Fruity
☐ Sour	☐ Bitter	☐ Strong	☐ Cloudy	☐ Citrus
☐ Acidic	☐ Yeasty	☐ Full-bodied	☐ Light	☐ Floral
☐ Cask	☐ Malty	☐ Watery	☐ Dark	☐ Chocolate
☐ Keg	☐ Wheat	☐ Clean	☐ Flat	☐ Toffee
☐ Bottle	☐ Spicy	☐ Balanced	☐ Fizzy	☐ Coffee

TASTING NOTES

Name:

Brewery:

Country of origin:

Style:

Where sampled:

Hops:

ABV:

IBU/bitterness:

SRM/color:

Notes:

Flavor profile:

☐ Sweet	☐ Hoppy	☐ Weak	☐ Clear	☐ Fruity
☐ Sour	☐ Bitter	☐ Strong	☐ Cloudy	☐ Citrus
☐ Acidic	☐ Yeasty	☐ Full-bodied	☐ Light	☐ Floral
☐ Cask	☐ Malty	☐ Watery	☐ Dark	☐ Chocolate
☐ Keg	☐ Wheat	☐ Clean	☐ Flat	☐ Toffee
☐ Bottle	☐ Spicy	☐ Balanced	☐ Fizzy	☐ Coffee

TASTING NOTES

Name:

Brewery:

Country of origin:

Style:

Where sampled:

Hops:

ABV:

IBU/bitterness:

SRM/color:

Notes:

Flavor profile:

☐ Sweet	☐ Hoppy	☐ Weak	☐ Clear	☐ Fruity
☐ Sour	☐ Bitter	☐ Strong	☐ Cloudy	☐ Citrus
☐ Acidic	☐ Yeasty	☐ Full-bodied	☐ Light	☐ Floral
☐ Cask	☐ Malty	☐ Watery	☐ Dark	☐ Chocolate
☐ Keg	☐ Wheat	☐ Clean	☐ Flat	☐ Toffee
☐ Bottle	☐ Spicy	☐ Balanced	☐ Fizzy	☐ Coffee

TASTING NOTES

Name:

Brewery:

Country of origin:

Style:

Where sampled:

Hops:

ABV:

IBU/bitterness:

SRM/color:

Notes:

Flavor profile:

- ☐ Sweet
- ☐ Sour
- ☐ Acidic
- ☐ Cask
- ☐ Keg
- ☐ Bottle

- ☐ Hoppy
- ☐ Bitter
- ☐ Yeasty
- ☐ Malty
- ☐ Wheat
- ☐ Spicy

- ☐ Weak
- ☐ Strong
- ☐ Full-bodied
- ☐ Watery
- ☐ Clean
- ☐ Balanced

- ☐ Clear
- ☐ Cloudy
- ☐ Light
- ☐ Dark
- ☐ Flat
- ☐ Fizzy

- ☐ Fruity
- ☐ Citrus
- ☐ Floral
- ☐ Chocolate
- ☐ Toffee
- ☐ Coffee

TASTING NOTES

Name:

Brewery:

Country of origin:

Style:

Where sampled:

Hops:

ABV:

IBU/bitterness:

SRM/color:

Notes:

Flavor profile:

- ☐ Sweet
- ☐ Sour
- ☐ Acidic
- ☐ Cask
- ☐ Keg
- ☐ Bottle

- ☐ Hoppy
- ☐ Bitter
- ☐ Yeasty
- ☐ Malty
- ☐ Wheat
- ☐ Spicy

- ☐ Weak
- ☐ Strong
- ☐ Full-bodied
- ☐ Watery
- ☐ Clean
- ☐ Balanced

- ☐ Clear
- ☐ Cloudy
- ☐ Light
- ☐ Dark
- ☐ Flat
- ☐ Fizzy

- ☐ Fruity
- ☐ Citrus
- ☐ Floral
- ☐ Chocolate
- ☐ Toffee
- ☐ Coffee

TASTING NOTES

Name:

Brewery:

Country of origin:

Style:

Where sampled:

Hops:

ABV:

IBU/bitterness:

SRM/color:

Notes:

Flavor profile:

- [ ] Sweet
- [ ] Sour
- [ ] Acidic
- [ ] Cask
- [ ] Keg
- [ ] Bottle

- [ ] Hoppy
- [ ] Bitter
- [ ] Yeasty
- [ ] Malty
- [ ] Wheat
- [ ] Spicy

- [ ] Weak
- [ ] Strong
- [ ] Full-bodied
- [ ] Watery
- [ ] Clean
- [ ] Balanced

- [ ] Clear
- [ ] Cloudy
- [ ] Light
- [ ] Dark
- [ ] Flat
- [ ] Fizzy

- [ ] Fruity
- [ ] Citrus
- [ ] Floral
- [ ] Chocolate
- [ ] Toffee
- [ ] Coffee

TASTING NOTES

Name:

Brewery:

Country of origin:

Style:

Where sampled:

Hops:

ABV:

IBU/bitterness:

SRM/color:

Notes:

Flavor profile:

- ☐ Sweet
- ☐ Sour
- ☐ Acidic
- ☐ Cask
- ☐ Keg
- ☐ Bottle

- ☐ Hoppy
- ☐ Bitter
- ☐ Yeasty
- ☐ Malty
- ☐ Wheat
- ☐ Spicy

- ☐ Weak
- ☐ Strong
- ☐ Full-bodied
- ☐ Watery
- ☐ Clean
- ☐ Balanced

- ☐ Clear
- ☐ Cloudy
- ☐ Light
- ☐ Dark
- ☐ Flat
- ☐ Fizzy

- ☐ Fruity
- ☐ Citrus
- ☐ Floral
- ☐ Chocolate
- ☐ Toffee
- ☐ Coffee

TASTING NOTES

Name:

Brewery:

Country of origin:

Style:

Where sampled:

Hops:

ABV:

IBU/bitterness:

SRM/color:

Notes:

Flavor profile:

- ☐ Sweet
- ☐ Sour
- ☐ Acidic
- ☐ Cask
- ☐ Keg
- ☐ Bottle

- ☐ Hoppy
- ☐ Bitter
- ☐ Yeasty
- ☐ Malty
- ☐ Wheat
- ☐ Spicy

- ☐ Weak
- ☐ Strong
- ☐ Full-bodied
- ☐ Watery
- ☐ Clean
- ☐ Balanced

- ☐ Clear
- ☐ Cloudy
- ☐ Light
- ☐ Dark
- ☐ Flat
- ☐ Fizzy

- ☐ Fruity
- ☐ Citrus
- ☐ Floral
- ☐ Chocolate
- ☐ Toffee
- ☐ Coffee

TASTING NOTES

Name:

Brewery:

Country of origin:

Style:

Where sampled:

Hops:

ABV:

IBU/bitterness:

SRM/color:

Notes:

Flavor profile:

- [ ] Sweet
- [ ] Sour
- [ ] Acidic
- [ ] Cask
- [ ] Keg
- [ ] Bottle

- [ ] Hoppy
- [ ] Bitter
- [ ] Yeasty
- [ ] Malty
- [ ] Wheat
- [ ] Spicy

- [ ] Weak
- [ ] Strong
- [ ] Full-bodied
- [ ] Watery
- [ ] Clean
- [ ] Balanced

- [ ] Clear
- [ ] Cloudy
- [ ] Light
- [ ] Dark
- [ ] Flat
- [ ] Fizzy

- [ ] Fruity
- [ ] Citrus
- [ ] Floral
- [ ] Chocolate
- [ ] Toffee
- [ ] Coffee

TASTING NOTES

Name:

Brewery:

Country of origin:

Style:

Where sampled:

Hops:

ABV:

IBU/bitterness:

SRM/color:

Notes:

Flavor profile:

⊔ Sweet	⊔ Hoppy	⊔ Weak	⊔ Clear	⊔ Fruity
⊔ Sour	⊔ Bitter	⊔ Strong	⊔ Cloudy	⊔ Citrus
⊔ Acidic	⊔ Yeasty	⊔ Full-bodied	⊔ Light	⊔ Floral
⊔ Cask	⊔ Malty	⊔ Watery	⊔ Dark	⊔ Chocolate
⊔ Keg	⊔ Wheat	⊔ Clean	⊔ Flat	⊔ Toffee
⊔ Bottle	⊔ Spicy	⊔ Balanced	⊔ Fizzy	⊔ Coffee

TASTING NOTES

Name:

Brewery:

Country of origin:

Style:

Where sampled:

Hops:

ABV:

IBU/bitterness:

SRM/color:

Notes:

Flavor profile:

- [ ] Sweet
- [ ] Sour
- [ ] Acidic
- [ ] Cask
- [ ] Keg
- [ ] Bottle

- [ ] Hoppy
- [ ] Bitter
- [ ] Yeasty
- [ ] Malty
- [ ] Wheat
- [ ] Spicy

- [ ] Weak
- [ ] Strong
- [ ] Full-bodied
- [ ] Watery
- [ ] Clean
- [ ] Balanced

- [ ] Clear
- [ ] Cloudy
- [ ] Light
- [ ] Dark
- [ ] Flat
- [ ] Fizzy

- [ ] Fruity
- [ ] Citrus
- [ ] Floral
- [ ] Chocolate
- [ ] Toffee
- [ ] Coffee

TASTING NOTES

Name:

Brewery:

Country of origin:

Style:

Where sampled:

Hops:

ABV:

IBU/bitterness:

SRM/color:

Notes:

Flavor profile:

☐ Sweet	☐ Hoppy	☐ Weak	☐ Clear	☐ Fruity
☐ Sour	☐ Bitter	☐ Strong	☐ Cloudy	☐ Citrus
☐ Acidic	☐ Yeasty	☐ Full-bodied	☐ Light	☐ Floral
☐ Cask	☐ Malty	☐ Watery	☐ Dark	☐ Chocolate
☐ Keg	☐ Wheat	☐ Clean	☐ Flat	☐ Toffee
☐ Bottle	☐ Spicy	☐ Balanced	☐ Fizzy	☐ Coffee

TASTING NOTES

Name:

Brewery:

Country of origin:

Style:

Where sampled:

Hops:

ABV:

IBU/bitterness:

SRM/color:

Notes:

Flavor profile:

- [ ] Sweet
- [ ] Sour
- [ ] Acidic
- [ ] Cask
- [ ] Keg
- [ ] Bottle

- [ ] Hoppy
- [ ] Bitter
- [ ] Yeasty
- [ ] Malty
- [ ] Wheat
- [ ] Spicy

- [ ] Weak
- [ ] Strong
- [ ] Full-bodied
- [ ] Watery
- [ ] Clean
- [ ] Balanced

- [ ] Clear
- [ ] Cloudy
- [ ] Light
- [ ] Dark
- [ ] Flat
- [ ] Fizzy

- [ ] Fruity
- [ ] Citrus
- [ ] Floral
- [ ] Chocolate
- [ ] Toffee
- [ ] Coffee

TASTING NOTES

Name:

Brewery:

Country of origin:

Style:

Where sampled:

Hops:

ABV:

IBU/bitterness:

SRM/color:

Notes:

Flavor profile:

☐ Sweet	☐ Hoppy	☐ Weak	☐ Clear	☐ Fruity
☐ Sour	☐ Bitter	☐ Strong	☐ Cloudy	☐ Citrus
☐ Acidic	☐ Yeasty	☐ Full-bodied	☐ Light	☐ Floral
☐ Cask	☐ Malty	☐ Watery	☐ Dark	☐ Chocolate
☐ Keg	☐ Wheat	☐ Clean	☐ Flat	☐ Toffee
☐ Bottle	☐ Spicy	☐ Balanced	☐ Fizzy	☐ Coffee

TASTING NOTES

Name:

Brewery:

Country of origin:

Style:

Where sampled:

Hops:

ABV:

IBU/bitterness:

SRM/color:

Notes:

Flavor profile:

☐ Sweet	☐ Hoppy	☐ Weak	☐ Clear	☐ Fruity
☐ Sour	☐ Bitter	☐ Strong	☐ Cloudy	☐ Citrus
☐ Acidic	☐ Yeasty	☐ Full-bodied	☐ Light	☐ Floral
☐ Cask	☐ Malty	☐ Watery	☐ Dark	☐ Chocolate
☐ Keg	☐ Wheat	☐ Clean	☐ Flat	☐ Toffee
☐ Bottle	☐ Spicy	☐ Balanced	☐ Fizzy	☐ Coffee

TASTING NOTES

Name:

Brewery:

Country of origin:

Style:

Where sampled:

Hops:

ABV:

IBU/bitterness:

SRM/color:

Notes:

Flavor profile:

☐ Sweet	☐ Hoppy	☐ Weak	☐ Clear	☐ Fruity
☐ Sour	☐ Bitter	☐ Strong	☐ Cloudy	☐ Citrus
☐ Acidic	☐ Yeasty	☐ Full-bodied	☐ Light	☐ Floral
☐ Cask	☐ Malty	☐ Watery	☐ Dark	☐ Chocolate
☐ Keg	☐ Wheat	☐ Clean	☐ Flat	☐ Toffee
☐ Bottle	☐ Spicy	☐ Balanced	☐ Fizzy	☐ Coffee

TASTING NOTES

Name:

Brewery:

Country of origin:

Style:

Where sampled:

Hops:

ABV:

IBU/bitterness:

SRM/color:

Notes:

Flavor profile:

- ☐ Sweet
- ☐ Sour
- ☐ Acidic
- ☐ Cask
- ☐ Keg
- ☐ Bottle

- ☐ Hoppy
- ☐ Bitter
- ☐ Yeasty
- ☐ Malty
- ☐ Wheat
- ☐ Spicy

- ☐ Weak
- ☐ Strong
- ☐ Full-bodied
- ☐ Watery
- ☐ Clean
- ☐ Balanced

- ☐ Clear
- ☐ Cloudy
- ☐ Light
- ☐ Dark
- ☐ Flat
- ☐ Fizzy

- ☐ Fruity
- ☐ Citrus
- ☐ Floral
- ☐ Chocolate
- ☐ Toffee
- ☐ Coffee

TASTING NOTES

Name:

Brewery:

Country of origin:

Style:

Where sampled:

Hops:

ABV:

IBU/bitterness:

SRM/color:

Notes:

Flavor profile:

- ☐ Sweet
- ☐ Sour
- ☐ Acidic
- ☐ Cask
- ☐ Keg
- ☐ Bottle

- ☐ Hoppy
- ☐ Bitter
- ☐ Yeasty
- ☐ Malty
- ☐ Wheat
- ☐ Spicy

- ☐ Weak
- ☐ Strong
- ☐ Full-bodied
- ☐ Watery
- ☐ Clean
- ☐ Balanced

- ☐ Clear
- ☐ Cloudy
- ☐ Light
- ☐ Dark
- ☐ Flat
- ☐ Fizzy

- ☐ Fruity
- ☐ Citrus
- ☐ Floral
- ☐ Chocolate
- ☐ Toffee
- ☐ Coffee

TASTING NOTES

Name:

Brewery:

Country of origin:

Style:

Where sampled:

Hops:

ABV:

IBU/bitterness:

SRM/color:

Notes:

Flavor profile:

☐ Sweet	☐ Hoppy	☐ Weak	☐ Clear	☐ Fruity
☐ Sour	☐ Bitter	☐ Strong	☐ Cloudy	☐ Citrus
☐ Acidic	☐ Yeasty	☐ Full-bodied	☐ Light	☐ Floral
☐ Cask	☐ Malty	☐ Watery	☐ Dark	☐ Chocolate
☐ Keg	☐ Wheat	☐ Clean	☐ Flat	☐ Toffee
☐ Bottle	☐ Spicy	☐ Balanced	☐ Fizzy	☐ Coffee

TASTING NOTES

Name:

Brewery:

Country of origin:

Style:

Where sampled:

Hops:

ABV:

IBU/bitterness:

SRM/color:

Notes:

Flavor profile:

☐ Sweet	☐ Hoppy	☐ Weak	☐ Clear	☐ Fruity
☐ Sour	☐ Bitter	☐ Strong	☐ Cloudy	☐ Citrus
☐ Acidic	☐ Yeasty	☐ Full-bodied	☐ Light	☐ Floral
☐ Cask	☐ Malty	☐ Watery	☐ Dark	☐ Chocolate
☐ Keg	☐ Wheat	☐ Clean	☐ Flat	☐ Toffee
☐ Bottle	☐ Spicy	☐ Balanced	☐ Fizzy	☐ Coffee

TASTING NOTES

Name:

Brewery:

Country of origin:

Style:

Where sampled:

Hops:

ABV:

IBU/bitterness:

SRM/color:

Notes:

Flavor profile:

- ☐ Sweet
- ☐ Sour
- ☐ Acidic
- ☐ Cask
- ☐ Keg
- ☐ Bottle

- ☐ Hoppy
- ☐ Bitter
- ☐ Yeasty
- ☐ Malty
- ☐ Wheat
- ☐ Spicy

- ☐ Weak
- ☐ Strong
- ☐ Full-bodied
- ☐ Watery
- ☐ Clean
- ☐ Balanced

- ☐ Clear
- ☐ Cloudy
- ☐ Light
- ☐ Dark
- ☐ Flat
- ☐ Fizzy

- ☐ Fruity
- ☐ Citrus
- ☐ Floral
- ☐ Chocolate
- ☐ Toffee
- ☐ Coffee

TASTING NOTES

Name:

Brewery:

Country of origin:

Style:

Where sampled:

Hops:

ABV:

IBU/bitterness:

SRM/color:

Notes:

Flavor profile:

- ☐ Sweet
- ☐ Sour
- ☐ Acidic
- ☐ Cask
- ☐ Keg
- ☐ Bottle

- ☐ Hoppy
- ☐ Bitter
- ☐ Yeasty
- ☐ Malty
- ☐ Wheat
- ☐ Spicy

- ☐ Weak
- ☐ Strong
- ☐ Full-bodied
- ☐ Watery
- ☐ Clean
- ☐ Balanced

- ☐ Clear
- ☐ Cloudy
- ☐ Light
- ☐ Dark
- ☐ Flat
- ☐ Fizzy

- ☐ Fruity
- ☐ Citrus
- ☐ Floral
- ☐ Chocolate
- ☐ Toffee
- ☐ Coffee

TASTING NOTES

Name:

Brewery:

Country of origin:

Style:

Where sampled:

Hops:

ABV:

IBU/bitterness:

SRM/color:

Notes:

Flavor profile:

- ☐ Sweet
- ☐ Sour
- ☐ Acidic
- ☐ Cask
- ☐ Keg
- ☐ Bottle

- ☐ Hoppy
- ☐ Bitter
- ☐ Yeasty
- ☐ Malty
- ☐ Wheat
- ☐ Spicy

- ☐ Weak
- ☐ Strong
- ☐ Full-bodied
- ☐ Watery
- ☐ Clean
- ☐ Balanced

- ☐ Clear
- ☐ Cloudy
- ☐ Light
- ☐ Dark
- ☐ Flat
- ☐ Fizzy

- ☐ Fruity
- ☐ Citrus
- ☐ Floral
- ☐ Chocolate
- ☐ Toffee
- ☐ Coffee

TASTING NOTES

Name:

Brewery:

Country of origin:

Style:

Where sampled:

Hops:

ABV:

IBU/bitterness:

SRM/color:

Notes:

Flavor profile:

- Sweet
- Sour
- Acidic
- Cask
- Keg
- Bottle

- Hoppy
- Bitter
- Yeasty
- Malty
- Wheat
- Spicy

- Weak
- Strong
- Full-bodied
- Watery
- Clean
- Balanced

- Clear
- Cloudy
- Light
- Dark
- Flat
- Fizzy

- Fruity
- Citrus
- Floral
- Chocolate
- Toffee
- Coffee

TASTING NOTES

Name:

Brewery:

Country of origin:

Style:

Where sampled:

Hops:

ABV:

IBU/bitterness:

SRM/color:

Notes:

Flavor profile:

▢ Sweet	▢ Hoppy	▢ Weak	▢ Clear	▢ Fruity
▢ Sour	▢ Bitter	▢ Strong	▢ Cloudy	▢ Citrus
▢ Acidic	▢ Yeasty	▢ Full-bodied	▢ Light	▢ Floral
▢ Cask	▢ Malty	▢ Watery	▢ Dark	▢ Chocolate
▢ Keg	▢ Wheat	▢ Clean	▢ Flat	▢ Toffee
▢ Bottle	▢ Spicy	▢ Balanced	▢ Fizzy	▢ Coffee

TASTING NOTES

Name:

Brewery:

Country of origin:

Style:

Where sampled:

Hops:

ABV:

IBU/bitterness:

SRM/color:

Notes:

Flavor profile:

- [ ] Sweet
- [ ] Sour
- [ ] Acidic
- [ ] Cask
- [ ] Keg
- [ ] Bottle

- [ ] Hoppy
- [ ] Bitter
- [ ] Yeasty
- [ ] Malty
- [ ] Wheat
- [ ] Spicy

- [ ] Weak
- [ ] Strong
- [ ] Full-bodied
- [ ] Watery
- [ ] Clean
- [ ] Balanced

- [ ] Clear
- [ ] Cloudy
- [ ] Light
- [ ] Dark
- [ ] Flat
- [ ] Fizzy

- [ ] Fruity
- [ ] Citrus
- [ ] Floral
- [ ] Chocolate
- [ ] Toffee
- [ ] Coffee

TASTING NOTES

Name:

Brewery:

Country of origin:

Style:

Where sampled:

Hops:

ABV:

IBU/bitterness:

SRM/color:

Notes:

Flavor profile:

☐ Sweet	☐ Hoppy	☐ Weak	☐ Clear	☐ Fruity
☐ Sour	☐ Bitter	☐ Strong	☐ Cloudy	☐ Citrus
☐ Acidic	☐ Yeasty	☐ Full-bodied	☐ Light	☐ Floral
☐ Cask	☐ Malty	☐ Watery	☐ Dark	☐ Chocolate
☐ Keg	☐ Wheat	☐ Clean	☐ Flat	☐ Toffee
☐ Bottle	☐ Spicy	☐ Balanced	☐ Fizzy	☐ Coffee

TASTING NOTES

Name:

Brewery:

Country of origin:

Style:

Where sampled:

Hops:

ABV:

IBU/bitterness:

SRM/color:

Notes:

Flavor profile:

- [ ] Sweet
- [ ] Sour
- [ ] Acidic
- [ ] Cask
- [ ] Keg
- [ ] Bottle

- [ ] Hoppy
- [ ] Bitter
- [ ] Yeasty
- [ ] Malty
- [ ] Wheat
- [ ] Spicy

- [ ] Weak
- [ ] Strong
- [ ] Full-bodied
- [ ] Watery
- [ ] Clean
- [ ] Balanced

- [ ] Clear
- [ ] Cloudy
- [ ] Light
- [ ] Dark
- [ ] Flat
- [ ] Fizzy

- [ ] Fruity
- [ ] Citrus
- [ ] Floral
- [ ] Chocolate
- [ ] Toffee
- [ ] Coffee

TASTING NOTES

Name:

Brewery:

Country of origin:

Style:

Where sampled:

Hops:

ABV:

IBU/bitterness:

SRM/color:

Notes:

Flavor profile:

☐ Sweet	☐ Hoppy	☐ Weak	☐ Clear	☐ Fruity
☐ Sour	☐ Bitter	☐ Strong	☐ Cloudy	☐ Citrus
☐ Acidic	☐ Yeasty	☐ Full-bodied	☐ Light	☐ Floral
☐ Cask	☐ Malty	☐ Watery	☐ Dark	☐ Chocolate
☐ Keg	☐ Wheat	☐ Clean	☐ Flat	☐ Toffee
☐ Bottle	☐ Spicy	☐ Balanced	☐ Fizzy	☐ Coffee

TASTING NOTES

Name:

Brewery:

Country of origin:

Style:

Where sampled:

Hops:

ABV:

IBU/bitterness:

SRM/color:

Notes:

Flavor profile:

- [ ] Sweet
- [ ] Sour
- [ ] Acidic
- [ ] Cask
- [ ] Keg
- [ ] Bottle

- [ ] Hoppy
- [ ] Bitter
- [ ] Yeasty
- [ ] Malty
- [ ] Wheat
- [ ] Spicy

- [ ] Weak
- [ ] Strong
- [ ] Full-bodied
- [ ] Watery
- [ ] Clean
- [ ] Balanced

- [ ] Clear
- [ ] Cloudy
- [ ] Light
- [ ] Dark
- [ ] Flat
- [ ] Fizzy

- [ ] Fruity
- [ ] Citrus
- [ ] Floral
- [ ] Chocolate
- [ ] Toffee
- [ ] Coffee

TASTING NOTES

Name:

Brewery:

Country of origin:

Style:

Where sampled:

Hops:

ABV:

IBU/bitterness:

SRM/color:

Notes:

Flavor profile:

- ☐ Sweet
- ☐ Sour
- ☐ Acidic
- ☐ Cask
- ☐ Keg
- ☐ Bottle

- ☐ Hoppy
- ☐ Bitter
- ☐ Yeasty
- ☐ Malty
- ☐ Wheat
- ☐ Spicy

- ☐ Weak
- ☐ Strong
- ☐ Full-bodied
- ☐ Watery
- ☐ Clean
- ☐ Balanced

- ☐ Clear
- ☐ Cloudy
- ☐ Light
- ☐ Dark
- ☐ Flat
- ☐ Fizzy

- ☐ Fruity
- ☐ Citrus
- ☐ Floral
- ☐ Chocolate
- ☐ Toffee
- ☐ Coffee

TASTING NOTES

Name:

Brewery:

Country of origin:

Style:

Where sampled:

Hops:

ABV:

IBU/bitterness:

SRM/color:

Notes:

Flavor profile:

☐ Sweet	☐ Hoppy	☐ Weak	☐ Clear	☐ Fruity
☐ Sour	☐ Bitter	☐ Strong	☐ Cloudy	☐ Citrus
☐ Acidic	☐ Yeasty	☐ Full-bodied	☐ Light	☐ Floral
☐ Cask	☐ Malty	☐ Watery	☐ Dark	☐ Chocolate
☐ Keg	☐ Wheat	☐ Clean	☐ Flat	☐ Toffee
☐ Bottle	☐ Spicy	☐ Balanced	☐ Fizzy	☐ Coffee

TASTING NOTES

Name:

Brewery:

Country of origin:

Style:

Where sampled:

Hops:

ABV:

IBU/bitterness:

SRM/color:

Notes:

Flavor profile:

☐ Sweet	☐ Hoppy	☐ Weak	☐ Clear	☐ Fruity
☐ Sour	☐ Bitter	☐ Strong	☐ Cloudy	☐ Citrus
☐ Acidic	☐ Yeasty	☐ Full-bodied	☐ Light	☐ Floral
☐ Cask	☐ Malty	☐ Watery	☐ Dark	☐ Chocolate
☐ Keg	☐ Wheat	☐ Clean	☐ Flat	☐ Toffee
☐ Bottle	☐ Spicy	☐ Balanced	☐ Fizzy	☐ Coffee

TASTING NOTES

Name:

Brewery:

Country of origin:

Style:

Where sampled:

Hops:

ABV:

IBU/bitterness:

SRM/color:

Notes:

Flavor profile:

- ☐ Sweet
- ☐ Sour
- ☐ Acidic
- ☐ Cask
- ☐ Keg
- ☐ Bottle

- ☐ Hoppy
- ☐ Bitter
- ☐ Yeasty
- ☐ Malty
- ☐ Wheat
- ☐ Spicy

- ☐ Weak
- ☐ Strong
- ☐ Full-bodied
- ☐ Watery
- ☐ Clean
- ☐ Balanced

- ☐ Clear
- ☐ Cloudy
- ☐ Light
- ☐ Dark
- ☐ Flat
- ☐ Fizzy

- ☐ Fruity
- ☐ Citrus
- ☐ Floral
- ☐ Chocolate
- ☐ Toffee
- ☐ Coffee

TASTING NOTES

Name:

Brewery:

Country of origin:

Style:

Where sampled:

Hops:

ABV:

IBU/bitterness:

SRM/color:

Notes:

Flavor profile:

- ☐ Sweet
- ☐ Sour
- ☐ Acidic
- ☐ Cask
- ☐ Keg
- ☐ Bottle

- ☐ Hoppy
- ☐ Bitter
- ☐ Yeasty
- ☐ Malty
- ☐ Wheat
- ☐ Spicy

- ☐ Weak
- ☐ Strong
- ☐ Full-bodied
- ☐ Watery
- ☐ Clean
- ☐ Balanced

- ☐ Clear
- ☐ Cloudy
- ☐ Light
- ☐ Dark
- ☐ Flat
- ☐ Fizzy

- ☐ Fruity
- ☐ Citrus
- ☐ Floral
- ☐ Chocolate
- ☐ Toffee
- ☐ Coffee

TASTING NOTES

Name:

Brewery:

Country of origin:

Style:

Where sampled:

Hops:

ABV:

IBU/bitterness:

SRM/color:

Notes:

Flavor profile:

- ☐ Sweet
- ☐ Sour
- ☐ Acidic
- ☐ Cask
- ☐ Keg
- ☐ Bottle

- ☐ Hoppy
- ☐ Bitter
- ☐ Yeasty
- ☐ Malty
- ☐ Wheat
- ☐ Spicy

- ☐ Weak
- ☐ Strong
- ☐ Full-bodied
- ☐ Watery
- ☐ Clean
- ☐ Balanced

- ☐ Clear
- ☐ Cloudy
- ☐ Light
- ☐ Dark
- ☐ Flat
- ☐ Fizzy

- ☐ Fruity
- ☐ Citrus
- ☐ Floral
- ☐ Chocolate
- ☐ Toffee
- ☐ Coffee

TASTING NOTES

Name:

Brewery:

Country of origin:

Style:

Where sampled:

Hops:

ABV:

IBU/bitterness:

SRM/color:

Notes:

Flavor profile:

- ☐ Sweet
- ☐ Sour
- ☐ Acidic
- ☐ Cask
- ☐ Keg
- ☐ Bottle

- ☐ Hoppy
- ☐ Bitter
- ☐ Yeasty
- ☐ Malty
- ☐ Wheat
- ☐ Spicy

- ☐ Weak
- ☐ Strong
- ☐ Full-bodied
- ☐ Watery
- ☐ Clean
- ☐ Balanced

- ☐ Clear
- ☐ Cloudy
- ☐ Light
- ☐ Dark
- ☐ Flat
- ☐ Fizzy

- ☐ Fruity
- ☐ Citrus
- ☐ Floral
- ☐ Chocolate
- ☐ Toffee
- ☐ Coffee

TASTING NOTES

Name:

Brewery:

Country of origin:

Style:

Where sampled:

Hops:

ABV:

IBU/bitterness:

SRM/color:

Notes:

Flavor profile:

- ☐ Sweet
- ☐ Sour
- ☐ Acidic
- ☐ Cask
- ☐ Keg
- ☐ Bottle

- ☐ Hoppy
- ☐ Bitter
- ☐ Yeasty
- ☐ Malty
- ☐ Wheat
- ☐ Spicy

- ☐ Weak
- ☐ Strong
- ☐ Full-bodied
- ☐ Watery
- ☐ Clean
- ☐ Balanced

- ☐ Clear
- ☐ Cloudy
- ☐ Light
- ☐ Dark
- ☐ Flat
- ☐ Fizzy

- ☐ Fruity
- ☐ Citrus
- ☐ Floral
- ☐ Chocolate
- ☐ Toffee
- ☐ Coffee

TASTING NOTES

Name:

Brewery:

Country of origin:

Style:

Where sampled:

Hops:

ABV:

IBU/bitterness:

SRM/color:

Notes:

Flavor profile:

- ☐ Sweet
- ☐ Sour
- ☐ Acidic
- ☐ Cask
- ☐ Keg
- ☐ Bottle

- ☐ Hoppy
- ☐ Bitter
- ☐ Yeasty
- ☐ Malty
- ☐ Wheat
- ☐ Spicy

- ☐ Weak
- ☐ Strong
- ☐ Full-bodied
- ☐ Watery
- ☐ Clean
- ☐ Balanced

- ☐ Clear
- ☐ Cloudy
- ☐ Light
- ☐ Dark
- ☐ Flat
- ☐ Fizzy

- ☐ Fruity
- ☐ Citrus
- ☐ Floral
- ☐ Chocolate
- ☐ Toffee
- ☐ Coffee

TASTING NOTES

Name:

Brewery:

Country of origin:

Style:

Where sampled:

Hops:

ABV:

IBU/bitterness:

SRM/color:

Notes:

Flavor profile:

- ☐ Sweet
- ☐ Sour
- ☐ Acidic
- ☐ Cask
- ☐ Keg
- ☐ Bottle

- ☐ Hoppy
- ☐ Bitter
- ☐ Yeasty
- ☐ Malty
- ☐ Wheat
- ☐ Spicy

- ☐ Weak
- ☐ Strong
- ☐ Full-bodied
- ☐ Watery
- ☐ Clean
- ☐ Balanced

- ☐ Clear
- ☐ Cloudy
- ☐ Light
- ☐ Dark
- ☐ Flat
- ☐ Fizzy

- ☐ Fruity
- ☐ Citrus
- ☐ Floral
- ☐ Chocolate
- ☐ Toffee
- ☐ Coffee

TASTING NOTES

Name:

Brewery:

Country of origin:

Style:

Where sampled:

Hops:

ABV:

IBU/bitterness:

SRM/color:

Notes:

Flavor profile:

- ☐ Sweet
- ☐ Sour
- ☐ Acidic
- ☐ Cask
- ☐ Keg
- ☐ Bottle

- ☐ Hoppy
- ☐ Bitter
- ☐ Yeasty
- ☐ Malty
- ☐ Wheat
- ☐ Spicy

- ☐ Weak
- ☐ Strong
- ☐ Full-bodied
- ☐ Watery
- ☐ Clean
- ☐ Balanced

- ☐ Clear
- ☐ Cloudy
- ☐ Light
- ☐ Dark
- ☐ Flat
- ☐ Fizzy

- ☐ Fruity
- ☐ Citrus
- ☐ Floral
- ☐ Chocolate
- ☐ Toffee
- ☐ Coffee

TASTING NOTES

Name:

Brewery:

Country of origin:

Style:

Where sampled:

Hops:

ABV:

IBU/bitterness:

SRM/color:

Notes:

Flavor profile:

- ☐ Sweet
- ☐ Sour
- ☐ Acidic
- ☐ Cask
- ☐ Keg
- ☐ Bottle

- ☐ Hoppy
- ☐ Bitter
- ☐ Yeasty
- ☐ Malty
- ☐ Wheat
- ☐ Spicy

- ☐ Weak
- ☐ Strong
- ☐ Full-bodied
- ☐ Watery
- ☐ Clean
- ☐ Balanced

- ☐ Clear
- ☐ Cloudy
- ☐ Light
- ☐ Dark
- ☐ Flat
- ☐ Fizzy

- ☐ Fruity
- ☐ Citrus
- ☐ Floral
- ☐ Chocolate
- ☐ Toffee
- ☐ Coffee

TASTING NOTES

Name:

Brewery:

Country of origin:

Style:

Where sampled:

Hops:

ABV:

IBU/bitterness:

SRM/color:

Notes:

Flavor profile:

- ☐ Sweet
- ☐ Sour
- ☐ Acidic
- ☐ Cask
- ☐ Keg
- ☐ Bottle

- ☐ Hoppy
- ☐ Bitter
- ☐ Yeasty
- ☐ Malty
- ☐ Wheat
- ☐ Spicy

- ☐ Weak
- ☐ Strong
- ☐ Full-bodied
- ☐ Watery
- ☐ Clean
- ☐ Balanced

- ☐ Clear
- ☐ Cloudy
- ☐ Light
- ☐ Dark
- ☐ Flat
- ☐ Fizzy

- ☐ Fruity
- ☐ Citrus
- ☐ Floral
- ☐ Chocolate
- ☐ Toffee
- ☐ Coffee

TASTING NOTES

Name:

Brewery:

Country of origin:

Style:

Where sampled:

Hops:

ABV:

IBU/bitterness:

SRM/color:

Notes:

Flavor profile:

☐ Sweet	☐ Hoppy	☐ Weak	☐ Clear	☐ Fruity
☐ Sour	☐ Bitter	☐ Strong	☐ Cloudy	☐ Citrus
☐ Acidic	☐ Yeasty	☐ Full-bodied	☐ Light	☐ Floral
☐ Cask	☐ Malty	☐ Watery	☐ Dark	☐ Chocolate
☐ Keg	☐ Wheat	☐ Clean	☐ Flat	☐ Toffee
☐ Bottle	☐ Spicy	☐ Balanced	☐ Fizzy	☐ Coffee

Notes

Notes

Notes

Notes

📓 Notes

Notes

Notes

Notes

PART THREE

Brewing Your Own

✳✳✳ ✳✳✳

Using the Recipe Pages

Use these pages to record any recipes you would like to brew at home. Below is an explanation of what goes in each part of the recipe chart:

Name	(Write the name of your beer)
Date	(Write the date that the brewing takes place)
Original gravity	(This refers to the weight of the beer before fermentation)
Water	(Record the amount of water that you will need for mashing and sparging)
Mash roll Weight	(Note the mixture of grains required to make up the "grain bill" or "mash roll" for mashing)

Mash schedule	(Note the amount of time you will need to leave your mash roll in the mash tun)
In the boil	Weight Time
	(Write the list of hop types, adjuncts, and finings you will need to boil up in the brewing wort)

Boil Duration	(Note the amount of time you will need to boil the ingredients in the brewing wort)
Yeast	(Note the amount and recommended type of yeast for the recipe)
Target FG	(This is the final gravity and refers to the weight of the beer after fermentation)
Target ABV	(Indicates the alcoholic strength of the beer)

RECIPE

★ ★ ★ ★

Name
....

Date
....

Original gravity
....

Water
....

Mash roll   Weight
....
....
....
....
....

Mash schedule
....

In the boil   Weight   Time
....
....
....
....
....

Boil Duration
....

Yeast
....

Target FG
....

Target ABV
....

Recipe

Name

Date

Original gravity

Water

Mash roll   Weight

Mash schedule

In the boil   Weight   Time

Boil Duration

Yeast

Target FG

Target ABV

Recipe

Name
....

Date
....

Original gravity
....

Water
....

Mash roll   Weight
....

....

....

....

....

Mash schedule

In the boil   Weight   Time
....

....

....

....

....

Boil Duration
....

Yeast
....

Target FG
....

Target ABV
....

RECIPE

★ ★ ★ ★

Name

Date

Original gravity

Water

Mash roll   Weight

_____

_____

_____

_____

_____

Mash schedule

In the boil   Weight   Time

_____

_____

_____

_____

_____

Boil Duration

Yeast

Target FG

Target ABV

RECIPE

★ ★ ★ ★

Name

Date

Original gravity

Water

Mash roll   Weight

Mash schedule

In the boil   Weight   Time

Boil Duration

Yeast

Target FG

Target ABV

Recipe

Name ....

Date ....

Original gravity ....

Water ....

Mash roll   Weight ....

....

....

....

....

....

Mash schedule ....

In the boil   Weight   Time

....

....

....

....

....

Boil Duration ....

Yeast ....

Target FG ....

Target ABV ....

Recipe

Name
....

Date
....

Original gravity
....

Water
....

Mash roll   Weight
....

....

....

....

....

....

Mash schedule

In the boil   Weight   Time
....

....

....

....

....

Boil Duration
....

Yeast
....

Target FG
....

Target ABV
....

RECIPE

★ ★ ★ ★

Name
_____

Date
_____

Original gravity
_____

Water
_____

Mash roll   Weight
_____

_____

_____

_____

_____

Mash schedule

In the boil   Weight   Time
_____

_____

_____

_____

_____

Boil Duration
_____

Yeast
_____

Target FG
_____

Target ABV
_____

RECIPE

★ ★ ★ ★

Name
_____

Date
_____

Original gravity
_____

Water
_____

Mash roll   Weight
_____

_____

_____

_____

_____

_____

Mash schedule
_____

In the boil   Weight   Time
_____

_____

_____

_____

_____

Boil Duration
_____

Yeast
_____

Target FG
_____

Target ABV
_____

Recipe

Name
Date
Original gravity
Water
Mash roll   Weight

Mash schedule

In the boil	Weight	Time

Boil Duration
Yeast
Target FG
Target ABV

Recipe

Name

Date

Original gravity

Water

Mash roll   Weight

Mash schedule

In the boil   Weight   Time

Boil Duration

Yeast

Target FG

Target ABV

RECIPE

★ ★ ★ ★

Name _____

Date _____

Original gravity _____

Water _____

Mash roll   Weight _____

_____

_____

_____

_____

Mash schedule

In the boil   Weight   Time _____

_____

_____

_____

_____

Boil Duration _____

Yeast _____

Target FG _____

Target ABV _____

RECIPE

★ ★ ★ ★

Name

Date

Original gravity

Water

Mash roll   Weight

Mash schedule

In the boil   Weight   Time

Boil Duration

Yeast

Target FG

Target ABV

Recipe

Name
....

Date
....

Original gravity
....

Water
....

Mash roll   Weight
....

....

....

....

....

....

Mash schedule

In the boil   Weight   Time
....

....

....

....

....

Boil Duration
....

Yeast
....

Target FG
....

Target ABV
....

Recipe

Name
....

Date
....

Original gravity
....

Water
....

Mash roll   Weight
....

....

....

....

....

....

Mash schedule
....

In the boil   Weight   Time
....

....

....

....

....

Boil Duration
....

Yeast
....

Target FG
....

Target ABV
....

RECIPE

Name
_____

Date
_____

Original gravity
_____

Water
_____

Mash roll   Weight
_____

_____

_____

_____

_____

_____

Mash schedule

In the boil   Weight   Time
_____

_____

_____

_____

_____

_____

Boil Duration
_____

Yeast
_____

Target FG
_____

Target ABV
_____

RECIPE

★ ★ ★ ★

Name

Date

Original gravity

Water

Mash roll   Weight

Mash schedule

In the boil   Weight   Time

Boil Duration

Yeast

Target FG

Target ABV

Recipe

Name
_____

Date
_____

Original gravity
_____

Water
_____

Mash roll   Weight
_____

_____

_____

_____

_____

_____

Mash schedule

In the boil   Weight   Time
_____

_____

_____

_____

_____

Boil Duration
_____

Yeast
_____

Target FG
_____

Target ABV
_____

Recipe

Name ....

Date ....

Original gravity ....

Water ....

Mash roll   Weight ....

....

....

....

....

....

Mash schedule

In the boil   Weight   Time ....

....

....

....

....

....

Boil Duration ....

Yeast ....

Target FG ....

Target ABV ....

RECIPE

★ ★ ★ ★

Name

Date

Original gravity

Water

Mash roll   Weight

Mash schedule

In the boil	Weight	Time

Boil Duration

Yeast

Target FG

Target ABV

RECIPE

★ ★ ★ ★

Name

Date

Original gravity

Water

Mash roll   Weight

Mash schedule

In the boil   Weight   Time

Boil Duration

Yeast

Target FG

Target ABV

Recipe

Name
....

Date
....

Original gravity
....

Water
....

Mash roll   Weight
....
....
....
....
....
....

Mash schedule

In the boil   Weight   Time
....
....
....
....
....

Boil Duration
....

Yeast
....

Target FG
....

Target ABV
....

Recipe

Name

Date

Original gravity

Water

Mash roll   Weight

Mash schedule

In the boil	Weight	Time

Boil Duration

Yeast

Target FG

Target ABV

RECIPE

Name

Date

Original gravity

Water

Mash roll   Weight

Mash schedule

In the boil   Weight   Time

Boil Duration

Yeast

Target FG

Target ABV

RECIPE

Name
_____

Date
_____

Original gravity
_____

Water
_____

Mash roll   Weight
_____

_____

_____

_____

_____

_____

Mash schedule
_____

In the boil   Weight   Time
_____

_____

_____

_____

_____

Boil Duration
_____

Yeast
_____

Target FG
_____

Target ABV
_____

Notes

Notes

Notes

Notes

Notes

Notes

PART FOUR

Keeping Organized

Favorite Bars and Pubs

Fill in the details of any bars or pubs you visit that serve great beer.

Name:

Address:

Website:

Phone:

Beers available:

Name:

Address:

Website:

Phone:

Beers available:

Name:

Address:

Website:

Phone:

Beers available:

Name:

Address:

Website:

Phone:

Beers available:

Name:

Address:

Website:

Phone:

Beers available:

Name:

Address:

Website:

Phone:

Beers available:

Name:

Address:

Website:

Phone:

Beers available:

Name:

Address:

Website:

Phone:

Beers available:

Name:

Address:

Website:

Phone:

Beers available:

Name:

Address:

Website:

Phone:

Beers available:

Name:

Address:

Website:

Phone:

Beers available:

Name:

Address:

Website:

Phone:

Beers available:

Name:

Address:

Website:

Phone:

Beers available:

Name:

Address:

Website:

Phone:

Beers available:

Name:

Address:

Website:

Phone:

Beers available:

Name:

Address:

Website:

Phone:

Beers available:

Name:

Address:

Website:

Phone:

Beers available:

Name:

Address:

Website:

Phone:

Beers available:

Name:

Address:

Website:

Phone:

Beers available:

Name:

Address:

Website:

Phone:

Beers available:

Name:

Address:

Website:

Phone:

Beers available:

Name:

Address:

Website:

Phone:

Beers available:

Name:

Address:

Website:

Phone:

Beers available:

Name:

Address:

Website:

Phone:

Beers available:

Name:

Address:

Website:

Phone:

Beers available:

Name:

Address:

Website:

Phone:

Beers available:

Name:

Address:

Website:

Phone:

Beers available:

Name:

Address:

Website:

Phone:

Beers available:

Name: _____

Address: _____

_____

Website: _____

Phone: _____

Beers available: _____

_____

_____

_____

Name: _____

Address: _____

_____

Website: _____

Phone: _____

Beers available: _____

_____

_____

_____

Name: _____

Address: _____

_____

Website: _____

Phone: _____

Beers available: _____

_____

_____

_____

Name: _____

Address: _____

_____

Website: _____

Phone: _____

Beers available: _____

_____

_____

_____

Name: _____

Address: _____

_____

Website: _____

Phone: _____

Beers available: _____

_____

_____

_____

Name: _____

Address: _____

_____

Website: _____

Phone: _____

Beers available: _____

_____

_____

_____

Favorite Brewers

Record the details of any notable brewers that come to your attention.

Name:

Address:

Website:

Phone:

Beers made:

Name:

Address:

Website:

Phone:

Beers made:

Name:

Address:

Website:

Phone:

Beers made:

Name:

Address:

Website:

Phone:

Beers made:

Name:

Address:

Website:

Phone:

Beers made:

Name:

Address:

Website:

Phone:

Beers made:

Name:

Address:

Website:

Phone:

Beers made:

Name:

Address:

Website:

Phone:

Beers made:

Name:

Address:

Website:

Phone:

Beers made:

Name:

Address:

Website:

Phone:

Beers made:

Name:

Address:

Website:

Phone:

Beers made:

Name:

Address:

Website:

Phone:

Beers made:

Name:

Address:

Website:

Phone:

Beers made:

Name:

Address:

Website:

Phone:

Beers made:

Name:

Address:

Website:

Phone:

Beers made:

Name:

Address:

Website:

Phone:

Beers made:

Name:

Address:

Website:

Phone:

Beers made:

Name:

Address:

Website:

Phone:

Beers made:

Name:

Address:

Website:

Phone:

Beers made:

Name:

Address:

Website:

Phone:

Beers made:

Name:

Address:

Website:

Phone:

Beers made:

Name:

Address:

Website:

Phone:

Beers made:

Name:

Address:

Website:

Phone:

Beers made:

Name:

Address:

Website:

Phone:

Beers made:

Name:

Address:

Website:

Phone:

Beers made:

Name:

Address:

Website:

Phone:

Beers made:

Name:

Address:

Website:

Phone:

Beers made:

Name:

Address:

Website:

Phone:

Beers made:

Name:

Address:

Website:

Phone:

Beers made:

Name:

Address:

Website:

Phone:

Beers made:

Favorite Beer Stores

A good beer store is a thing to treasure. Write down any great ones you come across and share the knowledge.

Name:

Address:

Website:

Mail order available:

Phone:

Breweries stocked:

Name:

Address:

Website:

Mail order available:

Phone:

Breweries stocked:

Name:

Address:

Website:

Mail order available:

Phone:

Breweries stocked:

Name:

Address:

Website:

Mail order available:

Phone:

Breweries stocked:

Name:

Address:

Website:

Mail order available:

Phone:

Breweries stocked:

Name:

Address:

Website:

Mail order available:

Phone:

Breweries stocked:

Name:

Address:

Website:

Mail order available:

Phone:

Breweries stocked:

Name:

Address:

Website:

Mail order available:

Phone:

Breweries stocked:

Name:

Address:

Website:

Mail order available:

Phone:

Breweries stocked:

Name:

Address:

Website:

Mail order available:

Phone:

Breweries stocked:

Name:

Address:

Website:

Mail order available:

Phone:

Breweries stocked:

Name:

Address:

Website:

Mail order available:

Phone:

Breweries stocked:

Name:

Address:

Website:

Mail order available:

Phone:

Breweries stocked:

Name:

Address:

Website:

Mail order available:

Phone:

Breweries stocked:

Name:

Address:

Website:

Mail order available:

Phone:

Breweries stocked:

Name:

Address:

Website:

Mail order available:

Phone:

Breweries stocked:

Name:

Address:

Website:

Mail order available:

Phone:

Breweries stocked:

Name:

Address:

Website:

Mail order available:

Phone:

Breweries stocked:

Name:

Address:

Website:

Mail order available:

Phone:

Breweries stocked:

Name:

Address:

Website:

Mail order available:

Phone:

Breweries stocked:

Name:

Address:

Website:

Mail order available:

Phone:

Breweries stocked:

Name:

Address:

Website:

Mail order available:

Phone:

Breweries stocked:

Name:

Address:

Website:

Mail order available:

Phone:

Breweries stocked:

Name:

Address:

Website:

Mail order available:

Phone:

Breweries stocked:

Name:

Address:

Website:

Mail order available:

Phone:

Breweries stocked:

Name:

Address:

Website:

Mail order available:

Phone:

Breweries stocked:

Name:

Address:

Website:

Mail order available:

Phone:

Breweries stocked:

Name:

Address:

Website:

Mail order available:

Phone:

Breweries stocked:

Name:

Address:

Website:

Mail order available:

Phone:

Breweries stocked:

Name:

Address:

Website:

Mail order available:

Phone:

Breweries stocked:

A Year In Beer

Record some of the best beers you drink in a year.

January	February	March
1		
2		
3		
4		
5		
6		
7		
8		
9		
10		
11		
12		
13		
14		
15		
16		
17		
18		
19		
20		
21		
22		
23		
24		
25		
26		
26		
27		
28		
29		
30		
31		

April

May

June

July	August	September
1		
2		
3		
4		
5		
6		
7		
8		
9		
10		
11		
12		
13		
14		
15		
16		
17		
18		
19		
20		
21		
22		
23		
24		
25		
26		
26		
27		
28		
29		
30		
31		

October

November

December

Notes